W9-BHS-512

MISSION CONTROL

MISSION CONTROL

HOW NONPROFITS *and* GOVERNMENTS CAN FOCUS, ACHIEVE MORE, *and* CHANGE THE WORLD

LIANA DOWNEY

bibliomotion
inc.

First published by Bibliomotion, Inc.
39 Harvard Street
Brookline, MA 02445
Tel: 617-934-2427
www.bibliomotion.com

Printed in the United States of America

Library of Congress Cataloging-in-Publication Data

Names: Downey, Liana, author.
Title: Mission control : how nonprofits and governments can focus, achieve
    more, and change the world / Liana Downey.
Description: First Edition. | Brookline, MA : Bibliomotion, 2016.
Identifiers: LCCN 2016002306 (print) | LCCN 2016006259 (ebook) | ISBN
    9781629561233 (hardback) | ISBN 9781629561240 (eBook) | ISBN 9781629561257
    (enhanced eBook)
Subjects: LCSH: Nonprofit organizations—Management. | BISAC: BUSINESS &
    ECONOMICS / Nonprofit Organizations & Charities. | BUSINESS & ECONOMICS /
    Structural Adjustment.
Classification: LCC HD62.6 .D69 2016 (print) | LCC HD62.6 (ebook) | DDC
    658/.048—dc23
LC record available at http://lccn.loc.gov/2016002306

For my family—I love you, a lot; and for all the leaders working hard to create a better world—those I have had the pleasure of working with, and those I have yet to meet, this one's for you.

CONTENTS

INTRODUCTION

It has been described as "one of the noblest and best things we have ever done as a species"—stopping one of humankind's most gruesome killers, globally feared and responsible for the deaths of more than half a billion people. It was an incredible feat. D.A. Henderson, an American physician and epidemiologist, led the charge to eradicate smallpox with the help of hundreds of thousands of people around the world, from illiterate workers in rural villages to specialist surgeons. It is hard today to grasp the scale of this undertaking, its urgency and importance. Very few of us remember or understand just how brutal and devastating smallpox was. This heroic feat required innovation and collaboration. But most of all, it required focus. After years of discussing the possibility, the World Health Organization set a ten-year goal in 1967 to eradicate smallpox—a goal known as Target Zero (zero cases of smallpox). The goal seemed outrageous—inconceivable. It was also spine-tingling and, critically, a goal focused on outcomes. "Target Zero...emphasized that the goal was not millions of vaccinations but zero cases of smallpox," noted Henderson.[1] Ten years later, the last known case of smallpox was recorded, and in 1980 smallpox was declared eradicated, saving sixty million lives and counting.

Why do some leaders succeed in changing the world while others struggle to point to their impact? What links the eradication of smallpox, the housing of one hundred thousand homeless Americans, and the dramatic reduction in drunk-driving fatalities? The leaders of these efforts shared a laser-like focus on their respective goals.

These leaders discovered the power of making the choice to be *something* to *someone*, rather than trying to be everything to everyone. Organizations that change the world share one critical feature. They systematically identify and target their efforts in their sweet spot—the intersection between what they are good at, what the world needs, and what works.

WHY ARE MISSIONS OUT OF CONTROL?

Does your organization lack focus? If so, you are not alone. Missions get out of control for three reasons. First, organizations are operating in an increasingly competitive funding environment. Second, many programs start by addressing symptoms rather than root causes. Finally, most social sector leaders have a hard time saying no. The result is mission creep, and with it, diluted impact and exhausted leaders.

The demand for nonprofit and public services is growing at an incredible pace around the world, but as the size of the sector grows, so does the competition for funding. This means many organizations follow the money. Perhaps an organization exists to raise funds for prostate cancer research, but finds out that there is a grant for raising awareness about the disease. The organization needs the resources, and this seems somewhat related, so without too much soul-searching it bids and succeeds. Over time, the organization's leaders continue to do this, adding services, and before they know it the nonprofit has moved from being a research-funding organization to being a direct-service, awareness-raising, lobbying, and research-funding organization. This is not inherently a bad thing, but if its initial focus was to research cures for prostate cancer, and its efforts have been pulled in multiple different directions, the result is mission creep, lost focus, and potentially diluted impact—and how much closer is a cure?

Many organizations start their lives with a narrow focus or activity in response to a clear need. Consider a food pantry. Perhaps a group of individuals in the local community notice that they have neighbors who are going hungry. They get together and start providing food to those in need. Before long, it becomes apparent that many of the people who are coming for food have other needs—housing, clothing, employment, and so on. So the food pantry starts offering referrals to homeless shelters and collecting clothing donations to give to its clients. They start providing job training. While all these activities are useful and worthwhile, what is not clear is whether this food pantry is the best organization to be meeting these needs. It has gone wide in its services, and certainly helped people along the way. But has this increase in the breadth of services enabled it to better meet the initial need? Are there still people in its community going hungry?

Considering root problems is wise. It is smart to make sure you are not just addressing a symptom (lack of access to food) if there is an underlying issue (unemployment) that in turn may be a symptom of an even deeper issue (lack of educational opportunities), and so on. It is worthwhile to go deeper and ask yourself if there is more you could be doing to address this issue. However, the problem is that most organizations do not prioritize their activities as a result of this thinking, but simply add one activity on top of the other. Instead of choosing to reallocate resources to higher-impact activities or referring clients with needs to other specialized organizations, most nonprofits and governments try to do it all and then create longer and more expansive mission statements to encompass all their work.

Finally, those of us who are drawn to work in the social sector do so because we care, and we care deeply. Many of us struggle with the idea of saying no to clients in need. While I admire and share this trait, this habit causes real problems. When you say yes to too many things your effort, focus, and energy are diluted, and so is your impact.[2]

WHAT'S THE SOLUTION?

So what's a leader to do? Work in the social sector is immensely more complex and challenging than strategy in the business world.

In business the goal is pretty clear—it usually boils down to maximizing shareholder value. This single focus makes it very simple to evaluate business ideas and prioritize activities. In general, businesses choose the ideas that are feasible and will generate the most profit. But things in the social sector are never that simple. Is it more important to teach literacy or social–emotional skills? How do you choose between two needy clients when you can only afford to serve one? Should you be expending resources on this program or another one? Many organizations lack the framework and structure from which to make these critical decisions. As a result, they end up overwhelmed, their resources stretched.

If you take only one thing away from this book, let it be this: impact comes from making thoughtful choices and *focusing your efforts*. To change the world you need a powerful strategy, and that requires you to make tough choices, not just about what you will do, but also what you will not do. It is time to take control.

Mission Control lays out a step-by-step process that will help you regain clarity and focus on what really makes a difference for your clients. Follow the steps, and you will find your focus and create a powerful strategy to help you make decisions, attract funding, and increase your impact.

WHY A BOOK AND WHY ME?

I hear from leaders on a regular basis that they need help. Many leaders are overwhelmed, under-resourced, and in desperate need of clarity and support. *Mission Control* is for all the leaders of nonprofits, social enterprises, and government who need help but are pressed for time and money.

I know how it feels. When I was younger I ran a national program for a large global nonprofit. We were trained in what was considered to be a well-thought-through planning approach, developed with the help of "expert" consultants. I sat through days and days of planning sessions. We worked incredibly hard—filled walls with pages of notes, completed the then-mandatory "SWOT" analysis (strengths, weaknesses, opportunities, and threats), and debated objectives late into the night. However, when I returned to day-to-day management, I remained unclear about what to focus on, what to say no to, and how best to direct the time and energy of my team. The mission was too broad, and our plan had too many goals. All the effort and time spent planning was a waste. Does that sound familiar? If so, you are not alone—hundreds of thousands of nonprofit and government leaders have similar experiences every year.

Years ago, I set out to crack this problem. I knew how powerful the right process could be for leaders like you. I have spent almost two decades studying, developing, implementing, and refining a simple, clear process for developing a powerful leadership strategy. I've worked with billion-dollar organizations, global NGOs, and federal, state, and city agencies around the world, and I have led planning for organizations of all sizes—from those with a staff of thirty thousand to fledgling agencies with just a few people and a dream of a better world. I was a leader of the government and nonprofit practices for McKinsey & Company and special strategic advisor to the Department of Prime Minister and Cabinet in Australia. Today I run an international firm with offices in the United States and Australia dedicated to helping organizations change the world. Our clients are tackling the most important issues of our day: equality, homelessness, conservation, education, employment, development, and justice. It is powerful and inspiring work. Many of our clients are stars in their field, but even stars need help every now and then.

Finding your focus is a bit like renovating a home: daunting, exciting, risky, and something you don't do every year. If the project goes wrong, you may not know until years later, when the cracks in the wall start to appear or the roof caves in. Of course, you could try to tackle it with no help, but that may be a very risky move.

That's where my team and I come in. We specialize in helping organizations have their "aha" moment, in orchestrating the instant a team finds its focus. I love those moments because they feel magical, but even more because they are the start of big things. Leaders with focus achieve more. I wrote *Mission Control* so you too, as a leader of a nonprofit, government, or social enterprise can implement proven approaches to help you find your focus, achieve more, and change the world.

HOW TO USE MISSION CONTROL

Mission Control is a step-by-step guide to developing a powerful strategy. The first chapter will help you **prepare for success** by assessing whether now is the right time to begin, who should be involved, how to get input, how long you should spend on the Mission Control process, and whether you should engage external support.

If and when you decide the time is right, begin! Each chapter presents a step in the process, complete with tools, examples, and, finally, answers to tough questions you may have—I call this the "cynic's corner." I recommend working your way through the book sequentially. While the process will almost certainly be iterative— you may find yourself coming back to earlier steps—the order is important. You can read the whole book before you begin the process but you do not have to. Just follow the steps as they are laid out.

To give you a feel for what lies ahead, here is a short overview of each of the remaining chapters.

The first step is to get the facts. You will learn how to identify, analyze, and gather the information you need to find your focus and identify certain facts you must know about your clients, your organization, and the sector in which you are operating. You will discover how to use this information to generate insights, and communicate them effectively so that all of your stakeholders are on the same page from the outset. Do not skip this step, even if you think you know most of what there is to know about your organization!

Next, you will set a spine-tingling goal. Distinct from a mission or vision, your goal will be a rallying cry and the focus for your work. By the end of this chapter you should have crafted a goal that will have you and your team leaping out of bed each morning, excited for the day ahead!

Once you have your goal, you will systematically *identify all options* available to help you reach it. You will learn techniques that will help you and your teams get creative and generate and organize ideas. Going broad will ultimately help you narrow in on the best path for reaching your goal.

Next, I show you some tricks for connecting with experts and the best research to help you *identify what works.* I share some examples of governments and nonprofits that skipped this step, and the unfortunate consequences. To avoid their fate, you will identify which of your options is most likely to work and under what conditions, which options are not likely to work, and which are untested.

Then you will *look inward* to identify your distinctive strengths and capabilities as an organization. This will help you identify which of the options you are best placed to pursue.

Then it is time to bring it all together and actually *choose* your path forward to inform your strategy. You will review your list of options, discarding ideas that do not have evidence behind them and those that are not well suited to your organization. You will focus instead on the ideas that have been shown to work and the ideas that you are best suited to pursue.

You will learn to *tell your story* in a way that is captivating, inspiring, and easy to understand. Your team, your funders, and your board will be able to clearly communicate your mission, goals, and strategy to increase funding and drive impact.

Finally, you will build an *action plan* so you can immediately get started on a path to achieve your goals and change the world.

❄   ❄   ❄

If you follow the simple steps in this book, you will soon be clear about your goal and how best to get there. With a focused strategy, your organization will be able to deploy your resources on the activities that matter the most.

Congratulations—you are on your way to developing a powerful, compelling strategy that will save you time, boost your impact, and maybe even change the world. Good luck!

1

PREPARE FOR SUCCESS

Before everything else, getting ready is the secret of success.[1]
—Henry Ford

The Mission Control approach is a step-by-step process to finding your focus and developing an action plan to increase your impact. You will learn how to gather and analyze critical facts about those you are serving, your organization, your sector, and the broader environment. You will find steps on how to set a spine-tingling goal, identify the full range of available options for achieving that goal, and prioritize your activities based on what works and what you're good at. You will craft a compelling story and develop an action plan to get you up and running. However, before you begin the Mission Control process, pause a moment and ask yourself these questions:

- Do we need more focus?
- Is now the right time?
- Whom should we involve?
- When should we involve people?
- How much time should we spend?
- Do we need a facilitator?

DO WE NEED MORE FOCUS?

Let's start with you. In your role as a leader or board member of a nonprofit or public organization:

- Do you ever feel overwhelmed or stressed, or have a sense of dread?
- Do you worry that you may not be able to deliver on many of the things people expect from you?
- Do you wish you could say no to some things, but are not sure how?

If you answered yes to any of these questions, then you need to get your mission under control. If not, then think now about your organization as a whole. Does your staff, team, or board ever:

- Find it difficult to describe the goal or goals of your organization clearly?
- Struggle to convincingly explain how your activities are going to achieve those goals?
- Lack confidence that you are reaching your goal or goals?
- Find it difficult to explain why you are pursuing some activities but not others?
- Find it challenging to choose among competing priorities like grant proposals?

If you answered yes to any of these—then you, too, could benefit from increasing your clarity and focus. You need *Mission Control.*

IS NOW THE RIGHT TIME?

I can be a world-class procrastinator. When faced with a tough task, I have been known to clean out the fridge, start learning a language, or convince myself that watching an episode of the *Real Housewives of Orange County* is really a learning opportunity. So if you are coming up with a list of reasons for why not to start, I can relate. However, there are really only two circumstances that should cause you to delay: when you are about to hire a new executive director or CEO, and when you are facing a major uncertainty. If your organization could benefit from more focus, then begin right away. The sooner you start, the sooner you will increase your impact and get some balance back in your life.

UNACCEPTABLE EXCUSES FOR WAITING

The following common excuses people give for delaying are not good reasons to wait.

I'm too busy. Typically, being busy is *not* a good excuse. Feeling busy and overwhelmed are often symptoms of a lack of focus. Thus, the sooner you complete the work described in *Mission Control,* the sooner you will feel more in control.

I don't have the money. This process is designed for those operating within tight budget constraints and does not require extra investment. Furthermore, having clarity about where you are headed and how you will get there will make you more compelling to funders.

We don't have a facilitator. You do not need one—this process is designed to be undertaken without an external consultant or facilitator.

We just did our planning! If you still lack focus, more work remains. You can certainly build on any planning work you have already done, but will stand to benefit from working through the chapters ahead.

GOOD REASONS TO WAIT

While the reasons just discussed are no justification for delay, there are, however, two circumstances under which you should wait.

You are about to hire a CEO or executive director. If you are part of a board of directors considering this process and are about to employ a new CEO or executive director, wait. The most attractive candidates—the people with real get-up-and-go—typically want to help shape the future of the organization. If you spend huge amounts of energy putting together a plan and then recruit a new leader, you will almost certainly have wasted time and energy. A new CEO wants to make her mark, and as a result often pushes back on key ideas overtly or (even worse) by stalling or subtly blocking suggestions. This is not a flaw—it is just human nature, and I have witnessed it plenty of times. Most leaders have a harder time getting excited about a direction or goal that they did not help shape. Therefore, hire first and get "Mission Control" second.

You are facing a major uncertainty. If you are waiting for a major uncertainty to resolve, it may be worth delaying—but only if there is a defined period after which you will get resolution. Examples include a big piece of legislation that might impact your work, a major funding decision, or a legal proceeding. The real world is complex and changing, so this process is flexible, but if waiting a short while (no longer than three months) will give you some clarity, then wait.

If now is not the right time to get started, there is still plenty you can do. Read and follow the steps laid out in the next chapter, "Get the Facts." Doing so will help improve your day-to-day management and position you very well for success once your CEO has been hired and/or your uncertainties have resolved.

STRATEGY FIRST, THEN STRUCTURE

In terms of sequencing with other activities, complete the Mission Control process before you do any restructuring or organizational design. It is a common mistake to put the cart before the horse and try to rearrange the organization before you know where you are going or what you will be working on. But how can you structure a team well if you do not know what you want them to do? Get a leader in place, and work out where you are headed and how you want to get there. Then, and only then, think about how your team should be structured to get you there.

WHOM SHOULD WE INVOLVE?

When it comes to involving others in the Mission Control process, the more the merrier—processes typically fail because they exclude some individuals, not because they include too many, or they falter because they wait too long in the process to engage people.

Not involving enough people is a mistake because almost everyone has some valuable input to share. Even those people you may not consider important stakeholders may possess information that could be critical to shaping a successful strategy. For example, they may know about upcoming policy shifts, the specifics of an issue facing the people you serve, or about innovations in your field. It is also a mistake because people who are not engaged tend to be much quicker to reject proposals. People use the degree to which they are consulted as an implicit measure of how important they are to the organization. If they feel that their opinions are not being sought they may start to disengage. I know of instances where funders have reduced or withdrawn their funding from an organization because they were not consulted on key decisions. A good strategy only has value if it can be implemented, so you should seek broad consensus, particularly amongst those responsible for doing the work. If you have found your focus and created a really smart, practical strategy to achieve your goals, but no one else is on board, you have wasted your time.

A Word on the Difficult Types

Inevitably, on any project, there are one or two individuals who have been identified as "difficult." You may even be explicitly advised to not talk to a particular person. Whenever I hear that, I politely dissent and then pick up the phone and invite that person to be part of the process. Why? Good question—I always cop an earful!

The "dissenters" inevitably have a bone to pick; they may have been passed over before, and it is likely that emotions are running high. They usually talk for a *long* time. But, there are three reasons you should reach out to them. One, I guarantee that they have thought long and hard about how things could be better. Once you get beyond the grousing, they are almost always a great source of insight. Two, if you find a way to work with them, they often become allies and advocates for change. Three, you'll regret it if you don't, because they will actively derail the process, vote no on principle, and generally find ways to make life difficult.

To ensure that their input moves from grousing to productive, you may need to help such people shift their mind-sets, rather than just involving them. Often, people who have been labeled difficult are really good at identifying problems, but they may not be as practiced at helping generate solutions. Or they may have a reputation as difficult because they are fierce advocates for a very small patch of the organization but are not in the habit of thinking about the whole organization. The best way to change this is to help them shift their vantage point and take on a different role. Ask them to solve for the whole, not their piece; ask them to start generating solutions rather than finding problems with solutions that others generate.

I find this is best handled candidly. For example, you might say, "You have thought about these issues so deeply, I am worried that without your input, we are not going to get the right answer. I don't want to be coming up with ideas without your help. Can you please help me develop a solution?" You can say (with a smile), "You have a reputation for being tough to convince. I am assuming that's because you think long and hard about things. The organization needs your brain, but we need it at work developing a better way forward, not just in picking apart any ideas other people come up with! Can you help us out and be part of the Mission Control team?"

Where there are multiple "difficult" people, so much the better—they become your working team. They can report to the board or the steering committee. The trick here is never to sideline people. Instead, make sure you put their frustrations, musings, and pent-up energy to work solving for the whole group.

WHO CARES?

Involving a wide range of people in the strategic planning process does not mean that you have to have every single person in the room for every step of the process. There are all kinds of manageable ways to solicit input, ensure that people feel engaged, and make sure everyone's voice is heard. Start by identifying the people with a stake in your organization (your stakeholders). For nonprofit organizations, these typically include:

- Board members (including national, local, and fundraising boards)
- Executives (CEO, head office, and program and regional leaders)
- Clients and supporters (e.g., children and their parents, animals and their owners, those with Alzheimer's and their carers, etc.)
- Funders (foundations, large donors) and relevant government agencies
- Other staff—including frontline staff (social workers, etc.)

You may also want to consider including:

- Academics with a specialization in your field
- Partner organizations and/or "competitors" (those you might see as fishing in the same funding pool you do)
- Client advocacy or umbrella groups

For government agencies, the list is similar, but with the addition of relevant political leadership (depending on your country and level of government: governor, mayor, ministers, etc.), other relevant political groups and nonprofits that fund you, and/or those that you fund to provide services.

Ask a few of the stakeholders you have identified above to also review the list and see who is missing. Inevitably, someone will think of a critical person or group that was somehow left off in the first round. As you start to engage people, make sure you keep asking the question: "Who else should we talk to?"

Once you have a list of your stakeholders, think about the capacities in which you might like to involve them. The first, and most useful, differentiation to make is whether you want people to have decision-making authority or to simply provide input. Note that some stakeholders—like the executive and board of directors—may have a legal responsibility to be involved in big strategic decisions. As long as you are very clear with people about their role from the beginning, they will usually understand that not everyone can or should be involved in making the final decision and they will appreciate your honesty. For example, you could convey the message to a

Stakeholder Group	Liaison	Status		Involvement		
		Survey	Interview	Decision Maker	Shared Brief	Consulted
Board	Iesha	✓	✓	✓	✓	✓
Executive staff	Iesha	✓	Some	✓	✓	✓
Clients	Ruth	✓	Some	Some	✓	✓
Client supporters	Ruth		Some		✓	
Major funders	Paul	✓	✓		✓	✓
Frontline staff	Iesha	✓	Some		✓	✓
Other staff	Iesha	✓			✓	✓
Academics	Paul	✓			✓	✓
Partners/comparable organizations	Paul	✓	Some		✓	✓
Client advocacy groups	Ruth	✓	✓		✓	

FIGURE 1.1   Stakeholder Checklist—Sample

local advisory board by saying, "We need and value your input and advice, but the national board will have the final say on our strategy." Figure 1-1 shows an example of a stakeholder checklist, showing who you will involve and how you will engage them.

It is important to note that the intent here is not just to placate people. You will have a better strategy if you listen to others (especially your clients) about the best way to have impact.

Of course, the wider you cast your net, the wider the different points of view will be. This can create a challenge, as you will almost certainly have conflicting perspectives but may still desire agreement. In order to help build consensus, keep these principles in mind—build from a fact base, ask questions, listen, demonstrate that you have heard and understood people's input, and be transparent. That means clearly communicating the choices open to you, your decisions and rationale along the way, and your final decision, as well as the reasons for the decision.

WHEN SHOULD WE INVOLVE PEOPLE?

Do not wait too long to involve people. Many executives I work with express the worry, "My boss/board/funders is/are so busy; I'd hate to bother them with something half baked." This sentiment is natural but it is also usually misguided. The result is that they wait a long time before sharing their thinking, and by the time they do share something they are often met with resistance.

Ironically, as I was writing this chapter I received a call from a frantic CEO of a nonprofit who was sharing that the recommendations from a very important review had not been approved by the board. As I probed, I learned that only a subset of the board had been actively involved in developing and reviewing the project along the way. People had been invited to give input, but the first time the whole board had engaged in detail was when they were asked to sign off on a finished set of recommendations. Not surprisingly, a third of the people said yes (do you think it was the people who had been more involved?), a third rejected the proposal, and the rest did not venture their opinions. So now, of course, the board has to go back and start again. This time, I am hoping the organization will be able to commit to a collaborative process and have people involved and engaged along the journey—so they can get to a shared decision about how to move forward.[2]

Involve people from the outset. Let people know you are *thinking* of undertaking a planning process, and that you would like them to be involved. Use a letter, an e-mail, or a phone call—anything is better than nothing. Provide some context: here's why we think this will help. In this initial communication, some questions you should ask are:

- Do you agree that such a review makes sense?
- Do you have any concerns about the timing?
- Would you like to be involved, and if so, how: would you be willing to be interviewed, participate in an online survey, and/or be part of a focus group discussion?
- Who else should we involve?

While you have their attention, it will be well worth your time to also get their input on what needs to change more broadly. Consider also asking:

- What would you like to see stay the same about the way we are working?
- What would you like to see change?
- What do you think we do really well?
- What should we improve on?

Be clear about where you are in the process (e.g., we haven't started yet!), and about any constraints (for example, whatever we do, we are not going to reduce our services to this client group; we are only dealing with the national strategy, not the international strategy).

Let people know key dates and when they can expect information and feedback. Let them know how you will keep them involved, stick to your time frame, and advise them of any changes.

Honest, frequent communication is your strongest ally here. In general, you will find it is easier to make frequent, pithy updates than to have big pauses with no information and then a mad dash to generate a comprehensive update.

HOW MUCH TIME SHOULD WE SPEND?

To complete all the steps as laid out in this book you will need enough time to gather facts, do research, consult your team, and have one or two longer meetings with your stakeholders. In general, you want to ensure you have enough time to do the work but not take so long that you lose traction. Three to four weeks is typically too short—I would say to aim for at least six weeks, and no longer than five months.

Other factors that will influence your timing include:

- The size of your organization and team—bigger teams usually need longer, because of the time involved in interviewing stakeholders, and so on.
- How much quality information you have at hand—the more you have, the less time you will need.
- The resources you have to support this process—is it just you in your spare time? Do you have a board subcommittee that can dedicate real time to this process? If you have fewer resources, you will need to spread the work out over a long period of time so as not to totally disrupt your day-to-day work.
- Any other big work or personal projects you have planned— are you moving offices? Getting married? Running a marathon? Plan accordingly and give yourself enough time!

Sometimes, especially in a big organization, you may have a longer time frame. When doing cascading work, for example, we've often done a piece where we work on a national focus and strategy over a four-month period, then work with each team to help them flesh out their part and get it much closer to being implementable—that whole process can take place over the course of a year but is run as multiple projects. Below, you will find a suggested time frame and plan for approaching your Mission Control process. You will notice that I recommend running two longer meetings or workshops, each about half a day in length. Over the years I have found this an effective way to maintain momentum while engaging decision makers. It gives you enough time to gather the facts and research you need to make good decisions, and the process is sufficiently open that people can have their say and make decisions together in the workshop setting. You should also continue to share pithy updates about your process and findings with your stakeholders throughout the process, say every week or two.

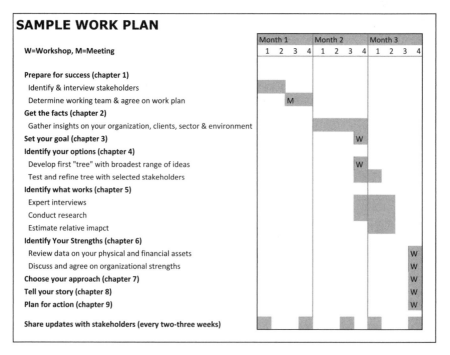

FIGURE 1.2   Sample Work Plan

DO WE NEED EXTERNAL HELP?

It is smart to ask whether you need external help in the form of a facilitator, advisor, or consultant. A big reason I wrote this book is to allow you to find your focus and without hiring a big team. However, you may well find that some *parts* of the process are easier if you have an objective and impartial advisor involved (this is particularly helpful for the steps covered in chapters 6 and 7, "Know Yourselves" and "Choose"). For those sections, you will find yourself way ahead of the game if you have actually done your homework and followed the advice laid out in this book.

The role of the facilitator will then be more about helping you to stay honest, and can be played by anyone who is objective, intelligent, a good listener, and willing to help out. This could be someone on your board or a friend of someone on your board (even better, as he will be more objective); it could even just be a friend of yours if you are a small team. Other organizations may be willing to help out by providing pro bono facilitation support (many good consulting firms will do this, and one day of support is a lot easier for them to provide than a full team and project). Having said that, there are times when the situation calls for more support and more help. If you decide you want more support, I would encourage you to read *Mission Control* through first, so you can understand the critical elements and identify where you think you may need support. Many of these steps you should be able to complete alone. If you decide to engage someone, it is worth considering the following.

WHAT A GOOD ADVISOR OR
FACILITATOR CAN DO

Of course not all advisors or facilitators are created equal, but the good ones should be able to help you with the following:

- Engage and consult with stakeholders
- Identify evidence-based practices to support you in your goals

- Track down and analyze internal and external data
- Synthesize results into insights
- Help you deliver your process on time
- Keep you honest—help you avoid making unsubstantiated claims about your assets, your impact, how effective your work is, and so on
- Ask questions that make you think twice, and provide sparks of insight
- Share approaches and strategies they have seen work in other organizations
- Introduce you to potential partners and supporters
- Help guide you to your own aha moments

WHAT AN ADVISOR OR FACILITATOR CANNOT DO

Even the best advisor cannot, and should not:

- Give you a great focus and strategy "from the outside in" (i.e., sit at her desk and write a plan for you)
- Do all the work for you (for example, find your data, put together your budget)
- Make decisions about what you should and should not focus on

WHAT TO LOOK FOR IN AN ADVISOR OR FACILITATOR

If you have decided that you would like to engage someone, here are the most important things to look for.

Does she have experience? As with anything, most consultants get better with time. Look for experience, not necessarily in your exact field (doing that may get you an answer that fits another organization, not yours), but in running strategic planning processes. Ideally, there is some convergence between strategic planning experience and content expertise—but at the end of the day, you and your team are the experts on your organization. A good consultant understands that, and is interested in bringing to the surface your expertise and wisdom and channeling it to help you make smart decisions.

Does he ask good questions? In any early conversations with a prospective consultant, keep your eye out for intelligent, thoughtful questions that generate insight and/or signal a real interest in getting to know you, your organization, the specific issues you are facing, and how best he can help.

Does she "get you"? It is important to have someone your team is going to feel comfortable with. Does the prospective consultant recognize the unique things about your team and your organization? If you have provided some context and background, has she read and absorbed it?

Does he speak in clear language? Be deeply suspicious of jargon. Someone who speaks only in obfuscating terms, referencing the latest trendy methodology or approach, but is unable to break those concepts down into clear, understandable language almost certainly does not understand them. Back away!

Will she plan with you or for you? A good plan is YOUR plan— you and your team believe in, understand, are excited by, and own it. Even though you are busy, do not make the mistake of thinking you can outsource all the work—a good consultant will guide you and support you, but at the end of the day, the plan should be yours. You should do real work to come up with a good one, even if you partner with a fantastic consultant. Any consultant who says, "We'll draft a plan for you to review," is not doing you any favors, no matter how busy you are.

Do his previous clients speak highly of him? Does she have long-term relationships with her clients? As in any industry, referrals are critical. Because it can be hard to know whether a strategy is sound until it has been implemented—and that usually means time has to have passed—long-term relationships speak volumes about how effective a consultant has been.

IN A NUTSHELL

Congratulations! You've asked yourself some tough questions, and I'm guessing you have decided your organization could use some Mission Control. You understand that this work of finding your focus should come before any reorganization work. Having determined that now is the right time for your organization, you are not going to procrastinate.

You have identified who should be involved and have possibly even started the process of reaching out to get their input. You have put together a time frame for the process and have thought about if and when you may need to get someone external involved. You are well set up to achieve Mission Control, find your focus, and increase your impact.

2

GET THE FACTS

The fewer the facts, the stronger the opinion.
—Arnold H. Glasow

"I am really worried. We know weight is a problem for lots of them, but it is getting really serious. One of the five-year-olds was just diagnosed with type 2 diabetes." As one staff member voiced her worry, others agreed: "They used to call it 'adult onset' diabetes, but not any more—it is really sad." Another team member asked, "What do you think—should one of our goals be to reduce obesity?" A murmur of approval rose from the group, before their boss interjected, "There's no point—it's impossible. Nothing works. Nothing has been shown to make a difference." Shoulders fell as hope deflated. The conversation almost stopped there and then, until one person asked, "Are we sure?" Their boss was confident, persuasive, articulate, and almost took the day. No one had any evidence to contradict his assertion, but he did not have evidence either. The group almost agreed to throw the idea out when someone spoke up. "Why don't we pause the conversation and do some research? Maybe we can reconvene in a few days." After a few days of phone calls and reading, the team learned of rigorous studies that showed there are interventions that work. In fact, two things make a big difference—limiting soft drinks and limiting screen time.[1] With the facts in hand, everyone, including the boss, easily agreed to tackle the issue.

Before you launch your first planning session, spend some time gathering basic facts about your clients, organization, sector, and environment. A common mistake that many organizations make is to assume that they already have a good understanding of the area in which they are working. They blithely head into a planning session armed only with a whiteboard, markers, and delicious snacks, instead of facts and opinions. This "fact-free" approach leads to a reliance on personal viewpoints, increases arguments, slows you down, and can lead to bad decision making.

In this chapter you will learn how to gather and clearly communicate critical information such as who your clients are, which other organizations are working in the sector, and which laws are most likely to impact your work. Following these steps and creating a fact base will help you make smarter decisions, drive consensus, and avoid unproductive arguments.

This part of the Mission Control process can be like eating your vegetables or exercising. It can be daunting, but you will feel virtuous and look great when you've done it!

To help you get moving, I have included only the most important questions about your clients, organization, sector, and the environment. You will also find tips on how to find and present factual information, and the end of each section explains why you want this information, highlighting the decisions it will help you make. There is also a short section on how to make powerful graphs and infographics to ensure that the information you have gathered is easily understood.

CLIENTS

Start with what matters the most, your clients. Assuming you have at least one client group, ask, who are they? What do they want? What are they like?

What Does the Term *Client* Refer To?

Throughout *Mission Control,* I use the term *clients* to refer to those your organization serves, a fairly common use in the nonprofit and governments sectors. This differs, of course, from the formal definition of a client as someone who pays for (and receives) services. In the social sector, these two are often disconnected: a funder may pay for a service received by a different client. If you are a social enterprise, you may have both paying customers and nonpaying clients, both of whom receive services as a result of your work. For example, Paul Newman's customers are the people who buy the spaghetti sauce, and its clients are the nonprofit organizations the company funds. In a buy-one-give-one model of social enterprise, customers are paying for their products, like glasses, shoes, or meals, but the clients are the ones getting a free pair of glasses or shoes, or the meal. Other organizations may also have a membership base—Amnesty International has members who act as funders and as volunteer activists, but their clients are the people they seek to protect from human-rights abuses.

WHO ARE YOUR CLIENTS?

Whom do you consider to be your clients? You may find that asking yourself this deceptively simple question sparks some soul-searching. If you work in justice, are you serving those incarcerated and released, their loved ones, victims of crime, or communities that want to be safe? If you are educators, are your clients children, parents, or future employers? If you are an environmental organization, do you consider your clients to be the animal and plant populations you are protecting, the land you want to protect, or the generations of people who will benefit from your conservation work?

You may also find that there is some discrepancy between the clients you are trying to serve and those you are actually serving. An executive director of a national nonprofit recently shared his experience of discovering that his organization's clients were actually a different population than the one it had intended to serve. While the initial purpose of the organization was to serve adult dyslexia sufferers, the staff learned through a fact-finding process that many of their clients are actually parents of children with dyslexia (only some of whom are dyslexic themselves). Understanding your client base will help you better target your efforts.

For this exercise, you should be writing down the clients you *want* to serve and noting any discrepancies between this list and the list of those you currently serve.

Presenting this information requires nothing fancy. Simply come up with as clear a definition as possible and write it down on one page. While you may want to debate and refine this definition as you go through the rest of this book, a draft is enough for now. Examples include:

- Refugees in Los Angeles
- Adult dyslexia sufferers in the U.S.
- Children at risk of dying from pneumonia, diarrhea, or malaria in West Africa
- Abandoned animals in Melbourne
- Music lovers in inner-city neighborhoods

WHAT DO YOUR CLIENTS WANT OR NEED?

While the rest of the chapter may be a bit like doing push-ups, identifying what your clients want is more like a pre-workout slice of chocolate cake. This is a generally inspiring thing to do, and answering this question should remind you of why you work so hard!

The best way to get this information is to directly ask your clients what they want and need. Unfortunately, many organizations are nervous about doing this. Just today I read a review of a new book about Facebook CEO Mark Zuckerberg's failed $100 million investment in schools reform in Newark, New Jersey.[2] The book blames the failure on a lack of consultation with the ultimate clients—students and their families. Zuckerberg is not alone. Many organizations just do not consult. Sometimes they fail to do this out of arrogance, assuming that clients do not know what they need.

Often, though, organizations hold back because of fear that asking the question will create all kinds of expectations that cannot be met. Sometimes, too, organizations fear that people, if asked, will want the "wrong things." However, research suggests that the opposite is actually true.[3] So, I encourage you to put aside a subtle bias that some well-intentioned boards, leaders, and staff suffer from, which is the sense that their clients may not know what they need.

Of course you should manage expectations and be clear about what you can and cannot do, but please, give your clients the benefit of the doubt and ask them directly what they want. Challenge yourselves to find ways to communicate directly with clients, even those with whom communication is difficult. Of course, despite your best efforts, there will be some instances where your clients simply cannot communicate their needs clearly. This will be the case if your clients are plants or animals, or if your clients are very young, infirm, or coping with other conditions that limit their ability to communicate. In the latter instances you should, where possible, talk to your clients' carers or make sensible assumptions.

If you already conduct client surveys, that's a great start. Check to be sure your surveys are sufficiently open-ended, and are not just asking, "How often are you attending our programs?" or "Are our programs working for you?" Those questions are important, but this exercise has a different purpose. You are looking to see if there are ideas that you are missing altogether from your work, or if you are prioritizing things that your clients would not. Ask your clients openly: "What are the top two or three things you want in life, and what do you want from us?" Both questions matter, because taken together the answers will provide a better picture of your clients' needs and how you can meet them.

If you do not conduct client surveys, there are many other ways to ask the questions. For example, you could: incorporate some extra time into client visits to ask these questions; call a sample of clients and ask for their input; invite a group of clients to come in for a snack and chat, and run a focus group; distribute surveys through the mail or online (using sites such as surveymonkey.com); or hit the streets with a clipboard or iPad and interview people directly.

To present this information, take some time to distill the key themes from conversations with clients, and provide illustrative quotes. Here's an example of what this can look like:

FIGURE 2.1   What Do Our Clients Want?

WHAT ARE YOUR CLIENTS LIKE?

How well do you know your clients? How many clients do you have and how does this compare to the population you could be serving? What other kinds of demographic information could help you better understand your clients and their needs? Where do they live? How old are they? How healthy are they?

How many clients do you have? If you think you know how many clients you have, make sure the number is valid. Check that you do not have clients who are deceased on your books, or are counting people multiple times because names and addresses have changed or are misspelled. For larger, more established organizations with databases your focus will likely be "cleaning" your data. This typically involves consolidating duplicate names and addresses and ensuring you do not have clients who are double-counted. If you don't have this information at all, do what you can; you may need to do a head count across programs, check for duplicates, and tally. For the purposes of this exercise a reasonable approximation is sufficient.

Keeping Track of Your Clients

If you are finding it difficult to track down even basic information like how many clients you have, this is a good time to think about how you can make the process easier in the future. Do you give your clients a unique identifier of some kind when they first connect with you? If not, you should start! It doesn't have to be sophisticated, but it should be consistent and easily comprehensible. You could use the clients' first and last names and the date you started to work with them.

If you serve people for just a few years of their lives, do you have a way of keeping in touch? This can be a big issue for organizations with clients who are transient, have literacy or language issues, or are grappling with poverty, but there are lots of ways to deal with this. I've seen organizations help set their clients up with an e-mail address on a common platform (Yahoo, Gmail, Hotmail, etc.) and provide some basic training about how to get online through a library. If a client has a cell phone, make sure you get the phone number, and then try to text or call your clients a couple of times a year to make sure the details are still current. This is also a good way to conduct short surveys and seek updates on how clients are doing if you are no longer serving them actively.

You can also offer incentives for clients to attend an annual focus-group meeting or check-in. You can create "alumni" groups of people who come through your program, and invest in building and maintaining supportive communities. This may be as simple as providing a meeting space, invitations, and some refreshments. If funds are tight, you can host an annual potluck gathering in a park and provide an information session as well as ensure you have current contact information for all attendees.

What is your reach? Comparing the number of clients you have with the overall population in need will determine your reach. You can use publicly available sources to estimate the size of your potential client base. For example, if you are an organization based in Texas and are looking to serve Alzheimer's sufferers, you could find out from the Alzheimer's Association that of the approximately 5.2 million people living in the U.S. with the disease, 330,000 of them are in Texas.[4] Your reach is then the total number of clients divided by the overall population, so if you are serving 10,000 people each year through your programs, then you are reaching 10,000 clients divided by 330,000 people in the target population, thus your reach is just about 3 percent. This can be shown as a simple pie chart or number.

What other demographic information would be helpful? Other demographic information can help you set sensible goals and find your focus. Use the table in Figure 2-2 to help you identify the two or three variables under your client type that will be most useful to you. The table is not exhaustive—if there's something else you think would be helpful, use that.

In addition to the suggested demographic information like age, there are a couple of questions at the bottom: How is this changing over time and how does this compare with the services we are providing? As in the example above, where we looked at reach, when you combine two pieces of information you often generate deeper insights. So once you have picked your two or three key questions, look both at how your client base has been changing over time and how this will affect the services you are providing. By way of example, here are two pairs of questions discussed in more detail: "How old are your clients and how has this changed over time?" and "Where do your clients live and how does this compare to where your services are located?"

■ *How old are your clients and how has this changed over time?* Age, and particularly changes in the age of your clients, can be of critical importance as you reflect on how relevant the mission of your organization is today. The National Council of

	People	Communities	Plants, Animals, or Environment
Demographics (pick two or three from the relevant list)	• Assets (skills, experience, networks) • Age • Location • Physical health • Mental health • Social networks • Income • Education and employment status & outcomes • Languages • Drug/alcohol use • Connection with justice system • Housing status • Marital status • Changes over time • Educational outcomes • Other?	• Assets (social networks, leaders/elders, events/arts, culture & history) • Age distribution • Access to services (healthy food, safe transport) • Educational/employment status & outcomes • Overall well-being (physical and mental health, disabilities) • Social networks • Crime & safety • Income distribution • Other?	• Distribution (where are they found?) • Health of plants/animals • Health of land (biodiversity, deforestation, soil quality, desalination, pollution, water quality and availability, air quality, etc.) • Risks/threats • Other?
	• How is this changing over time? • How does this compare to the services we are providing?		

FIGURE 2.2 Sample Demographic Questions

Jewish Women has members who support the organization as well as clients—those who are helped by the council. The membership base has changed significantly over time. Established when social and charitable organizations in the United States were segregated on the basis of race and religion, the council was founded to build community among Jewish women and provide opportunities for members to serve society more broadly. However, over time, as more women entered or remained in the workforce and other options for service opened up, the average age of the council's membership has increased substantially. For the New York office, getting the facts on how the age (and needs) of its membership base are changing has helped the board and executives reach agreement about how to focus their efforts and mission.

■ *Where do they live, and how does this compare to where your services are located?* If your organization works with disadvantaged populations, ensuring that clients have access to your services can be a real issue. Have you got services clustered in ways that made sense historically, but no longer serve the relevant populations? This can be particularly germane as populations age and neighborhoods gentrify, diversify, and change in other ways. Do your clients have to travel long distances to receive your services? Is this reducing the number of people you are serving? Are there other people who would benefit from your expertise if they could access services? One government department discovered a big discrepancy between where their childcare services were and where the families who needed those services most were living. While the centers were built in places of need initially, the neighborhoods had changed dramatically. Neighborhoods with the childcare centers did not have many young children, and vice versa. By plotting the centers and the demographic groups on a map, this point became very easy to see, and it was easier to convince the relevant decision makers of the need for change.

There are some great programs that map information to generate powerful insights. Following is an example from an online mapping tool called Policy Map (Policymap.com). This is just one selection from a large database of different kinds of information, and shows the percentage of Americans with a disability living in poverty by state. If you are a national organization with a focus on poverty and disability, for example, you could plot your own services against this map and identify any gaps in service or misallocation of resources. You can find links to this and other data and analysis tools at missioncontrolbook.com.

If you cannot find a service that has the information you need,

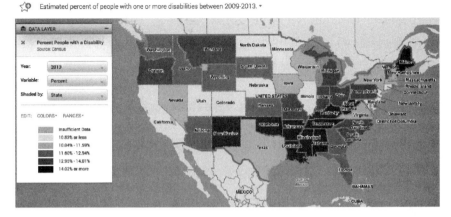

Estimated percent of people with one or more disabilities between 2009-2013.

FIGURE 2.3 Percentage of Population Living with a Disability, U.S. Map

sort your client data by zip code or neighborhood. That alone will help you better understand your distribution of services. Then use an application to create an online map (like ChartsBin.com—at the time of writing a free service—see missioncontrolbook.com for a more complete list). A good old-fashioned map with some red dots or pushpins can also be used to help you understand how your services line up with your clients' location.

Feeling Daunted?

If this feels like a lot, take a moment to remind yourself why you are doing this. Getting your facts straight at the outset will help you reduce unproductive arguments later. While at first it may seem reasonable to rely on your team's expertise, even the most intelligent and hardworking people are typically basing their opinions on their experience, which is obviously limited. Here is an example of the way conversations without a good shared fact base often unfold:

Executive director: Where should we be focusing our time?
Math specialist: We really need to increase the focus on math for our middle school students. Math is really important for long-term success.

> *Former high school principal:* I can see your point, but we really should focus our attention on graduation rates; the last two years of high school are key. Without graduating, kids have little chance of college or a career.
>
> *Early childhood specialist:* It's too late by then; we have to be doing more to support kids in the early years. I think we should invest in a new early-education approach that has had great success in other states.
>
> And so the conversation goes, with each leader absolutely convinced by the (good) points he is making, but in the absence of facts, this is a tough conversation to resolve. Getting your facts straight will reduce arguments and help you make smarter decisions.

You will use the facts you have gathered about your clients—who are they, how many you have, what they want, and other demographic information like changes in age and how the distribution of your services lines up with needs—in the coming chapters to help you set goals, prioritize, plan, and communicate with funders.

YOUR ORGANIZATION

How are you funded? How long could your organization go without new sources of funding? How many employees do you have? How many volunteers do you have? Gather some basic facts on your organization to help inform your choices.

Who is on your team? How many employees do you have? What kinds of work are they doing? Are they full time or part time? What about volunteers?

How are you funded? How much money have you raised, from which sources, and how has this changed over time? Here are two examples of ways to analyze and present this information:

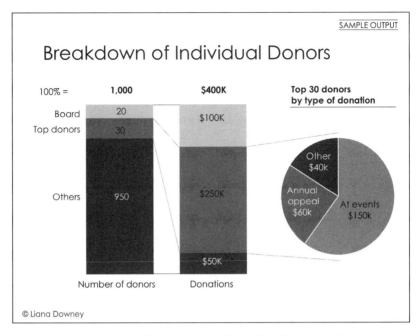

FIGURE 2.4   Example of Breakdown of Funding by Donor Type

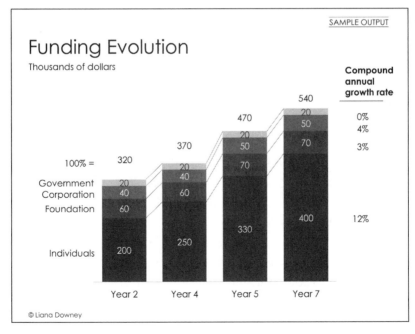

FIGURE 2.5   Example of Funding Evolution

How long could you go without new funding? How much cash on hand do you have today? If you raised no more money this year, how long would you be able to keep operating? (In simple terms, take the year's budget—let's say $1.2 million—and divide by twelve to get a monthly run rate of $100,000—that's how much you spend on average every month—and compare that to how much money is sitting in the bank or in accessible reserves. If you have $200,000 in the bank, then you have two months' worth of reserves.) In general, the more you have, the better protected you are.

What are your fixed costs? What costs do you have to pay no matter what? This might include permanent full-time staff, rent, or repayments on a long-term loan.

What are your variable costs? These are the costs that vary by how much activity you do (how many people you serve, how long you run programs for, or how many plays you put on, animals you shelter, patients you treat, and so on). Generally, your total costs are equal to the sum of your fixed and variable costs. It may be that some are a bit hard to define—that's okay, this is to give you a broad sense for how your cost base shifts as you grow your program.

What are your marginal costs? If you can, also try to estimate how much it would cost you to serve one more client. This is your *marginal cost,* and it is a very useful figure to know if you are thinking about doing something that would expand your program. For many organizations, this is not completely straightforward; for example, you may be able to work out how much it costs you to serve another three to four people (or shelter another animal, put on another play, etc.) but at some point you may need to add a new site or more staff, at which point the costs go up substantially. But asking these questions and having some idea of these costs can be very useful.

SECTOR

Your sector is simply the broad area in which you are working, such as animal rights, homelessness, education, early childhood, justice, or health. Some organizations work in multiple sectors, especially those that serve a specific client segment. For example, Children's Aid Society, a large New York City-based nonprofit, serves children across multiple sectors including education, housing, and health. Once you have identified your sector or sectors, you should determine: who else works in your sector and what they are doing; how the work is being funded; and the key government policies that impact your work and how those policies might change.

WHO ELSE IS IN YOUR SECTOR?

Who are the other players in your sector, and what are they doing? Who are their clients? What services do they provide? What new organizations and approaches have emerged in recent years?

This information can be gleaned from your existing networks and data—including your board, funders, and any staff or employees who have worked for other organizations—as well as by reading websites, social media sites, and the press. Look locally, nationally, and internationally. A quick way to do this is to brainstorm a list of organizations with your team and/or board and assign one person to each organization to learn more.

You may even be able to invite relevant people from similar organizations to talk with you about what they do. Far too often in the nonprofit sector there is intense competition among organizations, particularly when funding is limited. However, if you are indeed serving a similar goal or client group, it is all the more important to either collaborate or to make sure you are collectively addressing the gaps in services.

Here is a hypothetical example in the animal welfare space:

Name	Size ($m)	Animals served	Reach	Adoption	Foster	Shelter	Clinic	Current Partner
Humane Society	10	5,000	State	✓	✓	✓	✓	
Greyhound Love	0.5	10,000	County	✓	✓	✓	✓	✓
Red Dog Group	1	200	County	✓		✓	✓	
County Animal Services	90	40,000	County	✓		✓	✓	
ASPCA	170	40,000 (locally)	National	✓	✓	✓		

Columns 5–8 grouped under **Services**.

FIGURE 2.6   Sector Overview—Hypothetical Example

Once you have made this list you may want to think about what your relationships are like with these organizations. Are you actively competing with one another, or are you part of a coalition that has converged around a shared goal? How do other organizations measure their performance, and do they seem to be getting more traction than you?

If you are in government, make an effort to identify all the nonprofit organizations that are shaping policy and service delivery in your area (both those you work with today and those you do not). Investigate other groups doing similar work and serving similar clients in your city, state, and/or country. Much useful information can be gleaned simply by talking to counterparts in another state or department, as they are inevitably grappling with familiar issues.

Talk to Your "Competitors"

The possibility of speaking to others who are doing similar work to you, even if you are competing for funding, is one of the enormous benefits of being in the social sector. In the corporate sector this can be much harder—collaborating with other organizations on some topics is illegal! But in the social sector, you can get on the phone and learn what is working and what is not. People are often working on similar problems, and yet for all sorts of reasons (ego and concerns about funding being chief among them), this kind of communication does not always happen. There have been some notable exceptions of late, as some groups have explicitly pulled together to achieve certain goals. But you do not have to launch a huge "collective impact" initiative to learn from other organizations and strengthen your approach. Just pick up the phone, ask, and listen.

WHERE DOES THE MONEY COME FROM?

How is your sector funded? What (if anything) can you learn about where funding comes from? How much did the government spend in your sector? What foundations are actively supporting work in your field? This information can often be gleaned from aggregated sources such as the Nonprofit Finance Fund (nff.org), which surveys a wide range of nonprofits each year on funding trends. Sector umbrella groups may also be useful sources of information. If you can't find this information, it is not the end of the world, but having it will enable you to better target your fundraising efforts and understand how you compare to others.

WHO MAKES THE RULES?

Everyone operates in a policy context, and all organizations, especially governments and nonprofits, should have a good understanding of how policy impacts (or will impact) their clients and work.

The best way to get up to speed is to talk to relevant government representatives. Most departments have public-affairs officials whose job it is to keep the public up to date on policy and how best to work with government departments. Many countries also have great public-policy umbrella organizations that take responsibility for aggregating information on what is happening as well as helping shape policies. For example, umbrella groups in early childhood development in the United States include the National Association for the Education of Young Children (NAEYC) and the Association for Child and Youth Care Practice (ACYCP). In the affordable-housing sector, examples include the National Alliance to End Homelessness, Housing & Economic Rights Advocates (HERA), and others. (These are just a few examples from a very long list; for a more detailed list by sector and country, see missioncontrolbook.com.) If you are a member of an umbrella organization, invest some time in reading its publications, or if you are short on time, contact the group directly to ask for a summary of the key changes in your area. If you are not already a member, consider joining.

The questions you should be asking include:

- Which, if any, umbrella organizations represent your sector and/or your clients in lobbying discussions today?
- Which departments are responsible for monitoring, funding, and/or delivering services in your sector? (If you are a government department, think about other levels and branches of government—state, federal, departments versus elected representatives.)
- Who are the key decision makers in government (federal, state, and/or local)?
- What are the main laws that impact your clients, and are there any that may be revised (and do you want any of them revised)?

The facts you gather on your sector—who else is there, what are they doing, what is happening in funding and policy—will help you identify opportunities for collaboration and funding, ensure you are addressing service gaps rather than duplicating efforts, predict and respond to client needs, and identify ways in which you help shape policy and improve outcomes for your clients.

ENVIRONMENT

Finally, if you can, take a moment to look beyond your sector at the broader environment. What factors may impact your clients and your work? Consider economic, population, technology, or other sector-specific trends. I suggest you spend just a short period of time on this area (no more than a day) to ensure you do not get sidetracked by all the interesting developments that are out there. Another way to get some traction on this topic is to delegate the research to your board if you have one. Many board members may be grappling with similar questions in their day jobs, and by dividing and conquering the list of topics you may be able to pull together relevant information fairly quickly.

WHAT IS HAPPENING TO THE ECONOMY?

Big macroeconomic changes typically have huge ramifications for the government and nonprofit sector. An economic downturn can impact the social sector both through a rise in demand for services (as people lose jobs or hours) and through a decrease in available funding. Aim for a basic understanding of the latest forecasts for employment shifts and GDP growth.

HOW IS THE POPULATION CHANGING?

What other population trends could be relevant for your clients? Consider changes in the employment, age, migration, wealth, and/ or health of the population. Understanding employment trends, for example, may help you steer clients into training that is more likely to result in job placement, or may influence how you think about your fundraising strategy. Age, wealth, migration, and health trends can influence demand. For example, an aging population in many countries is putting pressure on senior service centers, demand for dementia carers, and the health-care system. In some cases, there are "baby booms" in specific demographic segments—Australia has experienced a rapid rise in births within indigenous communities, increasing demand for prenatal care in that community.

A good place to go for this kind of information is your national department or bureau of statistics. Most governments and many international development agencies conduct a census or survey on an annual basis, and these are fantastic repositories of useful information. In the United States, the website of the Census Bureau has a wide range of demographic information down to the individual zip code level at census.gov. In Canada, Statistics Canada can be found at statcan.gc.ca, while in the United Kingdom, the Office for National Statistics can be reached at ons.gov.uk, and so on.

HOW WILL TECHNOLOGY IMPACT YOUR WORK?

Technology is an ever evolving area with the potential to impact almost every facet of nonprofit and government operations. Technology has changed fundraising, increasing access to a wide array of small donors while simultaneously upping competition. The "ALS (amyotrophic lateral sclerosis) ice-bucket challenge" used peer pressure, eye-catching imagery, and social media to far exceed previous, more traditional fundraising efforts.[5] Technology is changing the way public campaigns are convened. For example, the movement "Moms for Gun Sense" mobilized millions of American mothers to successfully lobby for corporate and government policy changes in less than a year through well-crafted Facebook and Instagram feeds.[6]

Technology is also changing the way nonprofits and governments communicate and connect with clients. Governments are now tweeting and texting emergency warnings and event information, and gathering information and opinions on the impact of policies (such as policing, parking, and trash collection). Doctors and nurses are providing remote consultation and diagnostic services. Teachers and lecturers are providing massive open online courses (MOOCs) to huge global audiences. Surveys can be done almost instantly on tablets and smartphones. If you do not spend time reflecting on what technology could mean for you and your clients, you are missing major opportunities. Using these examples as a starting point, consider ways in which your sector, your clients, and your organization may be impacted by new technologies.

WHAT OTHER TRENDS WILL IMPACT YOU?

There may be other topics that are worth considering, such as climate change, global political shifts, wars, waves of refugees, currency crises, or trade agreements. Start with the output from your initial stakeholder conversations ("Preparing for Success") to see what trends people identified. Add to this information, and get some basic facts on any relevant trends. That way, when a well-meaning, articulate board member declares in your meeting that "climate change will be a huge issue," you can have a sensible, informed discussion about how climate change may or may not actually be a risk factor for your clients (e.g., risks of heat stroke in the elderly, wildfire risks threatening plant species), because you have done your research.

The information you have gathered on the broader environment—on economic, population, technology, and other trends—will help you anticipate and respond to changes in client demands, develop innovations in your services, target your activities and programs, and develop more realistic plans.

MAKE YOUR INFORMATION EASY TO ABSORB

You have worked hard to gather relevant data. You are not quite done with it yet! To reduce unproductive arguments and ensure you make smart decisions, you and your stakeholders must *understand* the information and its implications.

How you present your information matters tremendously. We worked with one client that initially would have said it was doing a great job with information. The organization certainly had a lot of data. Unfortunately, it was presented in small fonts in huge spreadsheets that had to be unfolded to read. As a result, no one was able to make much sense of the data, and I suspect no one really felt comfortable being the first one to say, "I don't understand all this information!" One of the things we did with the client's team was to identify the insights from the information and work with them to present it in clear charts. They told us that this simple change to the way the information was presented had a huge impact. The board and managers were finally able to make sense of the information—they could see underperformance and information gaps, and could identify differences in programs. As a result, they are able to make better decisions with fewer arguments, and, over time, improve outcomes.

To make sure your information is clear and understood, distill your research into a set of easy-to-understand insights. Then present this information in a clear and accessible way. That often means presenting information in a visual format, with just one message per chart.

To identify the insights from the data and analysis, ask yourself: What is the surprising or really important thing we have learned in this process? For example, perhaps looking at your information you noticed:

- You are only serving 3 percent of your target population.
- Your locations do not line up very well with the population you are serving.
- Your funding has been growing at a slower rate than your client base.
- Your work duplicates that of several other organizations but gaps in service still exist.
- Your clients are asking for help with employment but your work is focused on housing.

It's a good idea to keep one page where you gather these insights as you go through the process. A colleague of mine used to call it "flypaper"—it's the place where you just stick the insights that come up. Once you have all the insights identified, it is worth ordering these insights so that they tell a story. For example:

- We have only minimal reach into our client base, serving 3 percent of Texans with dementia (show chart), a segment that is forecast to grow rapidly over the next ten years (show chart).
- Our current sites are no longer well positioned to serve our client base (show map).
- Our funding is growing at a slower rate than demand from our clients (show chart), but we have increased funding from four core funders over the last five years (show chart).
- There may be an opportunity to partner with Organization X, which has sites in the areas where we are not currently located (show chart) and faces demand for our services (show chart).

Once you know what you want to highlight, you need to present the information in such a way that the insights leap from the page. You can start by doing a quick pencil sketch of how you want to present the information, for example what charts you might use (don't worry about having the data in there yet), and play around until you get something that makes the message immediately apparent.

Then present the information with one of the many easy-to-use charting tools that are out there. When I started working as a consultant (many years ago!), the ability to manipulate data and produce graphs from tables was a distinctive skill that we brought to clients. At times it could be a real production—we did complex analysis and used graphic designers to help draw the charts. Those days are long gone. Today, there are many tools and applications that make analyzing data and producing high-quality charts a breeze. Even my ten-year-old has put together graphs in Google Docs—usually as a way to persuade me I am being too stingy with pocket money. Many programs, including Excel, PowerPoint, Google Docs, and Pages, have easy-to-use charting functions, and there has been a proliferation of presentation and infographic apps (such as Infogr. am, icharts.net, and StatSilk.com—see missioncontrolbook.com for examples and links). But you cannot really go wrong with the basic chart functions in Excel/Numbers and PowerPoint/Keynote—they work well and are reasonably easy to use.

Finally, here are a few insider tricks from an old-time consultant to make your information easier to understand:

- Order it—if you have a chart that is designed to show order, spend two minutes with the information in a spreadsheet program like Excel—use the "sort by" function to sort it from highest to lowest, or vice versa—and then make the chart. It is much easier to interpret.

- Put your label as close to the information as possible; a legend can be super hard to follow, especially when there are lots of data points.

- Where possible, remove extraneous lines and other things that confuse charts.

- Include only one message or insight per page. Keep it simple.

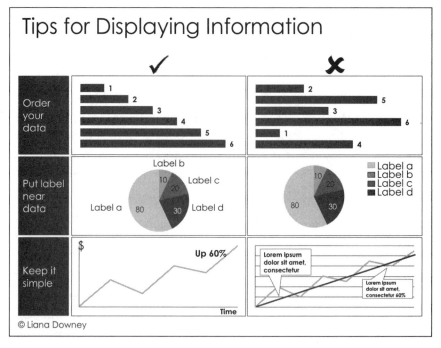

FIGURE 2.7 Tips for Displaying Data

Once you have a few useful analyses, you'll find you can keep coming back to them over and over. Your management team and your board (if you have one) can refer to them to understand trends, make decisions, and assess whether you are achieving your objectives.

Cynics Corner

I don't need to conduct research; my team will tell me what we need to know.

I am sure you have a great team that knows a lot about your organization. However, because most of us rely on observation to make decisions, we often get into the habit of thinking of observations as equivalent to facts. So, "It is my belief that..." becomes, "It is the case that...." Because most staff tend to engage with only a portion of the organization or a subset of clients, their observations are informed by only part of the relevant information. This is dangerous territory, because it means you may make decisions based on a subset of the facts. Getting the important facts will reduce arguments and streamline decision making.

Are you kidding me? I don't have time for this!

I get it, you're flat out, you don't have an analyst on staff, or you are just getting started, and so on. Here's the thing: if you start focusing your efforts (or if you are launching a new nonprofit) without a decent set of facts, you will almost certainly make some big assumptions, many of which will be wrong. You may spend years implementing a strategy based on hearsay, hunch, and instinct, and that is missing some critical pieces of information. Not only will that waste your time, your team's time, and your donors' time, but you may actually be making things worse. Do not kid yourself that just because you are smart, capable, and busy you can get away with putting together a fact-free strategy. Invest time here, and you will save time (and possibly lives) later.

While you do not need an analyst, if you are really finding it tough to do this investigation, you may want to contemplate getting some pro bono help from a university student. Many graduate schools have internship programs that offer students credit for working for a social enterprise, nonprofit, or government, and this kind of work is right up their alley. Relevant graduate programs include business, public policy, statistics, and information mapping. One example is Stanford's Alumni Consulting Team. Columbia's SIPA Program and Harvard's Kennedy School have similar programs. Contact the nearest university that offers a masters in public administration (MPA), masters in public policy (MPP), masters in public health (MPH), or masters in business administration (MBA) and ask if they have any such resources available.

I've started this process, and I'm just turning up a bunch of stuff I already knew!

First, congratulations; that's a good thing. You have a unique vantage point into your organization and your clients. You probably eat, sleep, and breathe your field and sector. However, do not assume everyone else has the same vantage point! Doing this work to get the facts will ensure that you are not missing anything, and it will also equip you to be more persuasive about how things stand with other critical stakeholders like funders, your board, and your clients.

Even if the first round of information is showing you what you already knew, I encourage you to look for hidden insights. Query the information in a few different ways in case there are things you did not know. For example, you may have already known that your clients are getting older—but perhaps your average male client is substantially older than your average female client. Perhaps much more of your funding comes from corporations now than it did ten years ago. Perhaps the government has launched a new program trying to do something very similar to what you are doing.

IN A NUTSHELL

Pat yourself on the back—you have just finished the most time-consuming section in the whole book. You've eaten your vegetables and done your sit-ups, and you look awesome! Everything gets easier from here.

You should now know about:

Your clients: who they are, what they want, and what they are like (including how many are served, where they live, key demographic information like their ages, and how these measures have changed over time)

Your organization: how many employees and volunteers you have, your fixed and variable costs, sources of funds and reserves

Your sector: who else is working to achieve similar goals, what they are doing, where the gaps are, who is providing funding, who the key players are in the policy arena, and how federal, state, and local policies are evolving

The environment: the trends that are likely to impact you and the population you serve

By identifying a key set of insights and putting together a pithy presentation, you will find it easier to create a shared understanding of the facts with your stakeholders. (I suggest you discuss your findings in the first of two workshops—see the appendix for a suggested workshop agenda.) This process may already have generated ideas about how you can refine your work to increase your impact. In the next chapters, use these insights to start setting goals and to focus on the key activities that are most likely to help you get there.

3

SET YOUR GOAL

I don't focus on what I'm up against.
I focus on my goals and I try to ignore the rest.
—Venus Williams

Where had we gone wrong? As an international nonprofit, we had a well-established brand. Our vision for "peace and the fulfillment of humankind's potential" was inspiring. We had brainstormed, discussed strengths, weaknesses, opportunities, and threats, and prepared a detailed work plan. Over the past year, we had increased membership and funding, received press coverage, run projects, and organized international exchanges. And yet, at the end of the day, it was nearly impossible to point to a specific impact we had made. Why? It took me years to figure it out, but ultimately the answer was simple. We were trying to be too many things to too many people. We were everywhere, and nowhere.

What brings you to work every day? What are you working toward? Are your stakeholders all pulling in the same direction? Focus matters. The exercises in this chapter will help you develop a clear and inspiring rallying cry for your organization. You should leave this chapter with a pithy, spine-tingling goal that will help you make decisions, motivate your team, and increase your impact.

You will notice I said goal, not mission. You may already have a mission. Missions tend to be expansive, not focused. They are wordy, often ambiguous and jargon-laden, and typically have very long-term horizons. I am going to go be controversial and say loud and clear that when it comes to helping you increase your impact, goals and values matter much more than missions. Missions may motivate, but they rarely are effective in helping you prioritize or make decisions. Your work in this chapter is very different from the usual process for developing a mission statement. There will be no committee struggling to agree on the third word in the second sentence. Your work is to develop a clear, focused one- to three-year goal.

Suggested Agenda for Workshop 1

Several of the exercises in this book should be done together with the decision makers you have identified. To that end, I often find the most effective use of everyone's time is to set aside two half days for workshops. In the first workshop you will complete the work in this chapter "Set Your Goal" and the next chapters "Identify Your Options."

Your agenda should include:

- Introductions and overview of objectives (15 minutes)
- Getting to know you exercise (30 minutes)
- Some discussion about desirable behavior for the day (e.g., all devices away, be candid, no interrupting, etc.) (10 minutes)
- A review and discussion about the facts you've gathered (you would send these out as prereading) (30-60 minutes)
- Set your goal (chapter 3) (30-60 minutes)
- Identify your options (chapter 4) (60 minutes)
- Confirm next meeting time and agree who will research which options are likely to work (chapter 5) (10 minutes)

If you think your board members may be unwilling to attend longer sessions, I would encourage you to ask! Despite many executive directors' reluctance to ask, boards will usually find a way to make the time. For them, a discussion about the long-term focus and future of the organization is almost always of interest. If setting aside three to four hours does prove impossible for your team, then you can run the process as a series of shorter meetings.

In this chapter, you will find a short overview of terminology (visions, missions, goals, and values), a discussion of why and how missions get out of control, and why goals matter more. Then you'll find the most exciting part, the three things that define a really good goal, and concrete steps to help you develop one of your own. I suggest you complete the work of this chapter and the next chapter in a workshop setting. See inset for a suggested agenda for this meeting. If you decide you can't get people for a longer workshop, then you will still want to set aside an hour or two to review the facts you have gathered and set your goal as a group.

TERMINOLOGY

Throughout this book, I will define vision as the end state you are working to achieve, a mission as the means to get there, goals as your interim steps to reach your vision, and values as the nonnegotiable aspects of the way you work.

Vision: the end state you are working to achieve (e.g., end hunger, world peace)

Mission: how you will get there (e.g., by distributing unused restaurant food, running a student exchange program)

Goal: clear, achievable steps to help you achieve your long-term vision and mission (e.g., halve the number of children who report coming to school hungry in Madison, Wisconsin; ensure that every participant in your exchange program this year leaves with positive feelings toward her host country)

Values: what is fundamental and distinctive about the *way* you work (e.g., clients treated with dignity, transparency in all our dealings, innovation, etc.)

Having said that, many organizations conflate these ideas into one statement. It actually doesn't matter. I'm not going to be messing with the wording of your mission or vision. My big learning over the last twenty years is that, while both a mission and vision can be inspirational to talk about, they are not the real differentiator between organizations that achieve great things and those that don't. Instead, organizations that create pivotal, lasting change are adept at setting and working toward highly focused, inspiring, and spine-tingling goals, and are supported by a consistent set of values. If you do not have a vision or mission, this process will help you work out what you want to do, and the result will be more useful than a classic mission statement. If you already have a mission statement, the process of setting a really concrete goal will help you tighten your work and get the mission under control.

REMINDER—WHY MISSIONS GET OUT OF CONTROL

In the introduction to this book, I noted that missions get out of control for three main reasons. First, people often start addressing a symptom and then move deeper as they better understand the cause. Second, they follow the funding. Third, they have a hard time saying no.

You may recall the example of a food pantry that starts by serving the needy and adds multiple services over time, potentially diluting the energy available to feed the hungry. This is a group that started with a symptom—hunger—and expanded its programs as staff better understood the root causes—like joblessness and lack of education—but did not actively reprioritize the group's efforts as a result.

You may also recall the prostate cancer organization that gradually adds services to meet highly specific grant requests, and ends up with a long list of programs that are not all pulling in the same direction. That organization, too, has a mission that lacks control.

Finally, we must acknowledge that many of us, myself included, find it difficult to say no to those in need. This is a problem, because we know that people perform better when they are able to concentrate their energy on a single goal.[1] Saying yes to too many things dilutes effort, focus, and energy, and dilutes impact.

So, many organizations lack focus. Yet organizations often work incredibly hard on missions and visions. Lots are developed with substantial input from the broader organization and then refined in long committee meetings. I suspect many of you have spent hours in lively debates trying to get the wording just right. Unfortunately, the result of this process tends to be more words, not fewer, and expansive rather than narrower objectives. Let's look at a few representative examples of mission statements:

■ We address complex, interconnected challenges facing our community as we implement our mission to: enhance the delivery of social services—particularly to the homeless, elderly, families, and children; increase the availability of quality housing to people facing poverty; foster economic revitalization; enhance educational and developmental opportunities for youth; and build community capacity through civic engagement.

■ We are a nonprofit, nonpartisan organization that strives to inspire broad participation in our democracy through the free exchange of ideas and civil dialogue and seeks to find ways to bridge the growing divisions that threaten our nation. We are dedicated to finding common ground and, through forums and initiatives, encourage the civic engagement so essential for a thriving democracy.

■ Our mission is to significantly improve the psychological, career, financial, and legal health and well-being of women, men, couples, and families, regardless of their ability to pay.

■ As a nongovernmental organization, our mission is to promote good health and healthy life styles in rural communities through health education, health literacy, capacity building, community engagement, research, and public health policy advocacy.

■ We are working to prepare all students for next-generation learning, work, and good citizenship by engaging schools, families, and communities in partnership through leadership, service, support, and outreach.

These are all worthy, inspirational statements. So what's wrong with them? They are too expansive, too hard to remember, and do not provide an effective framework for decision making. Each of these statements covers a huge amount of ground. The inclusion of a few prime pieces of jargon—"foster economic revitalization," for example—creates almost limitless possibilities for what could be included. Running a food pantry, teaching people to cook, running a computer class or a health clinic, launching a tech incubator, teaching a dance class, or painting a mural—there are arguments for why all of these could fit the mission. These missions make it almost impossible to say no. This expansiveness, combined with the fact that the statements are long and hard to remember (though not as long as some—UNICEF's fills a whole page), makes them almost useless as decision-making tools.[2]

COMPARING MISSIONS IN THE CORPORATE AND SOCIAL SECTORS

For those of you who are coming to the social sector with a corporate background, or who want to talk to stakeholders with a corporate perspective, I want to highlight some important differences between the role of a mission in the corporate and the social (nonprofit/government) sector.

My experience has been that mission statements tend to be more useful in the corporate sector, where they have a very different purpose. With profit as a clear decision-making factor, a mission is more about encouraging expansive thinking (away from a narrow product focus) and creating a sense of purpose for a team. In this context, a mission can be powerful for driving innovation and improving morale. The *Harvard Business Review* article "Building Your Company's Vision" notes that organizations that had a clear view of their mission (beyond just making money) were better able to rally and motivate their teams while also thinking expansively about their product offerings.[3] So for example instead of a Disney statement that says, "We make family-friendly cartoons," Disney employed the statement "We make people happy" to help them expand their thinking, allowing them to segue into theme parks, merchandise, and live-action movies. In this context, a mission really matters. It helps people feel connected to something bigger than themselves and find some meaning in their work.

However, in the social sector the majority of staff already find meaning in the work they are doing.[4] That's not the problem. The issue, in their case, is not the absence of an inspiring mission— the issue is typically that they have *too expansive* a mission. Without a concrete goal around which they can rally, measure impact, and feel progress, they feel too great a burden for all the ills in the world, and burnout is a common result. Indeed, 78 percent of non-profit workforce said they feel "used up" at the end of the day, and more than half suggested they were looking for a new role.[5]

So this chapter is not about your mission statement. Instead, it is dedicated to setting a goal—a clear, spine-tingling goal. It may be that this goal defines the work of your organization only for the next few years, and if so, good. Far better to make real strides in the next few years in a particular area, achieve the goal, and set another, than to continue to work incredibly hard in multiple directions and only make incremental change.

FEATURES OF A POWERFUL GOAL

A powerful goal articulates an achievable end state, is clear, and is spine-tingling. When you hear it, you want to know more, and you want to get involved.

IT SHOULD HAVE AN ACHIEVABLE END STATE

Your goal must articulate an end state—so that you know when you have achieved it. To give you an example, "Save the environment" may be an inspiring and worthwhile objective, but it is a mission, not a clear goal. How do you know when the environment is saved? A goal to "Stop the dumping of industrial solvent in Wisconsin waterways," "Stop whale hunting," or "Reduce U.S. methane emissions by 20 percent" is much more specific. While these goals may still be difficult to achieve, they clearly articulate an end state. With these kinds of goals, you will know when you are finished.

IT SHOULD BE CLEAR

Lack of clarity is a huge issue for most nonprofits. I think it has something to do with those of us who are drawn to social-sector work—as I noted earlier, we are not in the habit of saying no. Many of us feel uncomfortable making choices, especially when it means someone may not receive something he needs, and as a result many organizations include a very wide range of activities in their goals and missions.

We may also fall back on slightly ambiguous terms as a way to avoid making a decision. For example, one of the missions above included the phrase to "build community capacity through civic engagement." Terms like "community capacity" and "civic engagement" are not uncommon in the social sector, and most people would say yes, I know what that means. But do we really have a clear understanding of the term? What defines civic engagement—happiness, involvement in decision making, voter turnout, employment rates, or attendance at community events? What defines community capacity—income levels, education, social networks, or health? This lack of focus only serves to diffuse effort and often impact. Power comes from making tough choices now, which will help make choices in the future easier. Clarity comes both from the focus that the goal articulates and through simple language that is easily understood.

IT SHOULD BE SPINE-TINGLING

The goal should give you butterflies. Here's a goal: "To double the number of children reading at grade level by the end of the year."

Does it tell you where you are going? Yes. Will you know when you have achieved it? Yes, you will. Is it clear? Reasonably. But is it spine-tingling? Not really. Let's look at a version that is.

This is one of my favorite examples of a goal that meets all three criteria, borrowed from Dan and Chip Heath's great book about what it takes to make sustained change, *Switch: How to Change Things When Change Is Hard.*[6] A teacher, Crystal Jones, faced with an incoming first-grade class that was really struggling, many failing to meet basic literacy and school readiness standards, set an audacious goal for her class: to be "third graders by the end of her year."

That is pretty powerful. Especially for the kids. Would they know when they got there? Yes, they would, because there are clear standards laid out for what it means to be working at a third-grade level. Was it clear? Absolutely? But more importantly, was it spine-tingling? You bet—particularly if you are a first grader who knows just how big and impressive those third graders can be!

Here's another great goal from one of my clients, Community Solutions. They set (and ultimately surpassed!) the incredible and absolutely spine-tingling goal of "100K Homes."[7] That is, the organization set a goal to house one hundred thousand Americans, focusing particularly on the most vulnerable, those who had been homeless for many years. This powerful goal became the rallying cry for more than 250 organizations all around the country, each of which identified the piece that it could influence. Because the 100K Homes campaign team did such a fantastic job of tracking, measuring, and sharing results, what had initially seemed like an incredible stretch goal gradually became reality. People pooled their energy, talent, and intellect to remove what had previously seemed insurmountable obstacles and achieved amazing things.

Now that you have a sense of the features of a great goal, how do you set your own? I suggest you follow a few key steps, which I will expand upon in the next few pages.

- Develop a short list of outcomes you are seeking for your clients
- Narrow the list down

- Set some boundaries
- Set a target
- Consider your time frame
- Plan to celebrate progress

DEVELOP A SHORT LIST OF DESIRED OUTCOMES

Think about the real change you are seeking in your work. What is a single outcome that would give you cause for celebration? Here are some examples to get you started:

Animal welfare/environment
- A plant/animal is no longer on the endangered species list
- An animal is safely adopted
- A piece of land is protected
- Water is clean enough to safely drink
- A source of pollution is removed

Health/safety
- Survival rates from a disease improve
- There is an increase in life expectancy
- There are no gun deaths this year
- There are no deaths from domestic violence
- There is a big reduction in the incidence of a disease
- There are no deaths from a disease, medical error, traffic accidents, etc.
- Assaults decrease
- There is a reduction in the number of suicides

Early childhood
- A child meets key development milestones
- A baby is breastfed for twelve months
- A child is being read to daily

Education/disadvantage
- A student graduates from college
- A person stays out of jail
- A person gains employment
- A person is no longer living in poverty
- A person is housed (or still housed)
- A person increases her support networks
- Children are not reporting being hungry
- Inequality decreases

The Arts
- A production is critically acclaimed
- A production or piece of art leads to an increase in awareness about a particular issue (poverty, racism, inequality, corruption, etc.)
- A differently abled child attends a music class and experiences an increase in well-being
- Children learn to dance and their health improves

Public transportation
- Disadvantaged families pay less than 5 percent of their income to commute to work
- Pollution from car use is reduced
- People can commute between work and home safely

These are just examples to get you started. If your type of organization is not listed above, I hope you still find some inspiration. Note that examples are simple and focus on the outcome of the work rather than the delivery of your service.

NARROW IT DOWN

You will be able to identify many important outcomes, but to be effective you need to find a way to focus, and narrow down your list. Choose the outcome that will have the biggest difference for your clients.

THE ARGUMENT FOR FOCUS

I know it is easier said than done, but focus matters. When Mothers Against Drunk Driving was founded in 1980, its singular focus on eliminating drunk driving in the United States gave the organization absolute clarity.[8] There are about sixteen thousand fewer fatalities per year (which more than halved the fatality rate) since MADD launched its program.[9] Focus allows you to concentrate your resources so that you get better at delivering for your clients. It will help you break the cycle you may be in of chasing after funding, diluting your efforts, and getting distracted. By concentrating your efforts, you will be able to deliver better results. And when you really start to demonstrate impact, you will immediately become a more attractive funding proposition.

Do your best to pick just one goal. If you do end up with more than one goal, bear in mind that, to be effective, you probably really need to have a team structure that reflects your multiple objectives. For example, if you have three goals, you should have three separate teams, each working toward a different goal. Perhaps you should even have three different organizations. While you can choose to plan together as a group, you will still need to develop three distinct action plans, because the ways in which you are achieving these goals will be very different. Remember this if you find yourselves saying, "We can't narrow it down." Ask yourselves if you will have more impact choosing one goal and really delivering it or having multiple goals and achieving lukewarm results on all of them. If you do achieve your goal in the next few years then you simply set the next, more ambitious target. Onward and upward!

HOW TO NARROW DOWN YOUR LIST OF GOALS

Ask your clients (if you can) what they would most like to achieve. Ask yourselves the same question: If your organization could only deliver one thing for your clients, what would you choose? It may be worth doing a quick poll—often you quickly find alignment around one goal, or at least a shorter list emerges.

Ask if you are better positioned to deliver on some than on others. Or are there some needs that no one else is meeting? For example, one of my clients was trying to determine whether it should focus on crime reduction or job creation, the top priorities expressed by members of the community. There was already another organization focusing on crime reduction, so the team decided to concentrate its efforts on job creation, where it saw a gap.

Once you've got a shortlist, spend time as a team (or as a leader) imagining how it will feel if you make real strides in achieving each of these outcomes. How would it feel for your clients, your team, for you? How would the community you are serving be changed by these successes? Choosing your goal should involve your mind and your heart. What resonates with you and your team? What energizes you? What goal could you fall in love with? As a wise man once noted, "What you are in love with, what seizes your imagination, will affect everything. It will decide what will get you out of bed in the morning, what you will do with your evenings, how you will spend your weekends, what you read, who you know, what breaks your heart, and what amazes you with joy and gratitude. Fall in love, stay in love and it will decide everything."[10] This applies not just to people, but to our choices in our work too.

In my experience there is an almost mystical moment, when the group knows what is right. The energy in the room rises substantially and the answer suddenly feels obvious. While I am firm in my belief that one should not follow the heart in terms of *how* you reach your goal (see the following chapters), in terms of picking the goal, if you have done all the legwork I suggested, now is the time to trust your instincts. Which goal gives you butterflies? Which goal could you love?

If questions remain, then pick your top two (or three), and push on with the rest of the stages in this book. As you move through the exercises you will start to identify your sweet spot—where a gap exists and where you have the biggest potential to make a difference. That is where you should focus your efforts.

SET SOME BOUNDARIES

Now that you have identified a goal, set some boundaries or parameters, for example around which groups you will serve or in what geographies you will work. The hard work you put into getting the facts justifies itself because you now know the clients you are working with, what they want, and who else needs your services.

Categories to consider include geography, age, gender, ethnicity, health, wealth, and immigration status. Are you going to focus your efforts on a particular city or state? Will you work only with the young or elderly? Get as specific as possible to help avoid future ambiguity. For example, instead of "We help recently released prisoners find work," try "All female prisoners in the state of New Hampshire are employed six months after release."

SET A TARGET

For many organizations, the real rallying cry comes from setting a goal that feels truly audacious, a little bit on the edge of reason, and a little bit frightening! To do that requires being specific about the scale of impact you want to have. There is nothing like setting an exciting target to pull people together—"Eradicate smallpox," "End malaria deaths," and "100K Homes" are powerful examples. If relevant, attached numbers to your goal. You may have heard of the notion of a "Big Hairy Audacious Goal," a term popularized by Jim Collins and Jerry Porras in *Built to Last*.[11] While they were focused more on the power of twenty- to thirty-year goals for corporations, their findings apply equally to the social sector: it's very motivating to have a goal that makes you stand up and take notice. So be courageous with your goal. Give people something to get really excited about, something big and game changing.

People are also motivated by traction, so consider picking a goal for which you can already show some results, or wait to announce a goal until you have some. (However, I do not suggest you tie people's performance reviews to the goal—see chapter 9, "Plan for Action," for more details.) Strive to find a balance between a number that is challenging and one that is ultimately achievable.

Make sure you build from your facts. Do not just pluck a number out of thin air, but work from your research or do more, if necessary. For example, when I was working with Community Solutions on the launch of a new campaign—"5000 jobs for Brownsville"—the team looked at all the facts before we set a target for new jobs created. They looked at how many people were out of work in the community, how old they were, and where they lived. They looked at education levels of the community, at employment statistics, and at the success of other job creation programs. This helped the team set a sensible number and also informed the strategies they pursued.

TIME SPAN

It is also important to have a clear time frame within which you want to achieve your goal. It can be a long time if your goal is really bold. You'll need to decide whether it would be better to give yourselves another year but get a higher number, or to achieve a smaller number in a shorter time frame.

How long you give yourself to achieve your goal will be influenced by other factors, often beyond your control. For example, when I was leading a student nonprofit, members left when they graduated from university, which meant that we lost a third to a quarter of our volunteer workforce every year. As such, we set annual goals. For government organizations, you may want to set goals that line up with political term limits, since everything tends to shift when parties change. Consider having a soft launch of a goal—get some traction first, then announce your goal and your progress to date at the same time.

CELEBRATE PROGRESS

Your team needs to see and celebrate progress toward your big goal. I cannot emphasize this point enough! Track progress, post results for all to see (in your office, on your website) and have celebrations for getting partway. Doing this will help you maintain morale and build momentum.

VALUES

Early in this chapter I touched on the importance of defining your values. These are two to three nonnegotiable aspects of the way you work. When people think of you, they should naturally think of these values (like treating clients with dignity, being fact-based, or listening). Your values should be synonymous with your people and approach. Here are some simple ways to identify your values:

- Think of someone who best represents your organization (and/or what it aspires to be), and list the values that person demonstrates. Pick only two or three at most from the list.
- Ask people to review the list of values in appendix 3 and identify the ones they personally relate to the most, then ask them to do the same for the organization.
- You can also download and complete the list of values at missioncontrolbook.com.

Do not pick too many values—the more you have, the less meaningful they will be. Once you have identified your values, they only become real if they really do define the *way* you work. In addition to modeling the values—that is, behaving in a way that is consistent with the values—you can ensure they become part of the organization's daily practice by talking about them on a regular basis, but even more powerfully by building them into the way you recruit and manage people. You should look to hire people who embody the traits you value and assess people's behavior against these values.

Cynics Corner

But we already have a mission statement, and getting agreement on it was exhausting! There's no way I can get my stakeholders aligned around another set of goals.

Your goals should be aligned with your mission statement. They will not necessarily replace your mission statement in discussions with donors about who you are and what you do, but unless your mission statement is so focused and defined that it helps you make decisions on a day-to-day basis, you need something else. A powerful goal, particularly one with a two- to three-year time horizon, will help you head in the right direction and get a lot closer to achieving your mission. After setting your goal you and your stakeholders may notice issues with your mission statement—length, jargon, expansiveness. Fortunately, working through the Mission Control process will clarify the issues that need to be fixed and make it much easier to rein in your statement.

We cannot possibly narrow our focus—if we do, we will leave clients behind.

Are you achieving all for your clients that you would like today? Can you confidently claim that you are making a real impact? If you are then you probably don't need this book! However, if, like many social-sector organizations, you deliver a load of services but cannot confidently speak to their impact, then you may already be leaving your clients behind. By saying no to some activities you will be free to embrace other, more important activities more fully.

But we have teams that are focused on work that we haven't prioritized—what will those people do?

Unfortunately, you will probably need to rethink your organizational structure. If you have teams that are focused on work that, after a good hard think, doesn't seem to be a real strategic priority, then you should redeploy those teams to the work that is. Or, like some of my clients, you may decide that it is better to let another organization focus on work that you no longer prioritize, and there may be an opportunity to transfer some funding, and/or some of your team members to work for that other organization. If you are not confident you are being effective and having real impact, then go through each of the steps outlined in this book, get your strategy in place, and then reconfigure your organization to support your strategy. But whatever you do, you should not let your current structure dictate your strategy. It may be painful, but it will make a huge difference in the long run.

IN A NUTSHELL

Once you have completed the work in this chapter you will have chosen a clear, spine-tingling goal, one that is focused on the outcomes that will make the biggest impact in your clients' lives. You should feel inspired and excited. If your goal makes you a little nervous, that's a good sign—it shows you have been courageous. Note that this is the second important choice of three that you will make. You first chose who you would serve—your clients—and now, with your goal, you have chosen what you will help your clients achieve. In the following chapters you will review the various options for achieving that goal. You will identify and prioritize those that you are best placed to implement and the ones that are the most likely to succeed. This will be your third and final choice—how you will reach your goal.

4

IDENTIFY YOUR OPTIONS

No idea is so outlandish that it should not be considered.
—Winston Churchill[1]

I am about to share one of the most powerful techniques I have learned in my career—how to systematically break a challenging problem into manageable pieces. I wish someone had taught me this in school. It would have made me a better student and a better nonprofit leader. I had a consulting colleague who loved this approach so much that he advocated applying it to any and every problem he could think of. Which neighborhood should he live in? How could he get to the airport on time when traffic is backed up? What would it take for his girlfriend to get back together with him? I did tease him about the latter (maybe less time spent problem solving and more time with her?), but he was on to something. This approach is powerful. I had a client at a large education department who had been chipping away at a problem for ages—how to ensure students were college- and career-ready. When I sat down to work through it with him, we applied this approach and came up with some new ideas and a structure. He said, "This is so much better than what I had before. Why is that?" Well, the secret is in how you break the problem down—and you're about to learn how.

You have a bold, spine-tingling goal. Now is the time to think courageously about how to achieve it. This is your chance to step back and contemplate all the different paths open to you. At this moment, do not be limited by your first idea or your current activities, or say no to ideas that may seem outlandish. While I will show you a structure to guide your thinking, feel free to be expansive and let your imagination run free.

In this chapter you will learn how to use an option tree to identify, organize, and analyze a wide range of options that will help you achieve your goal. Only once you have a complete list of options should you start to think about how to narrow it down.

"Trees" in various formats—decision trees, issue trees, profit trees—are a form of diagram widely used in engineering, manufacturing, and business. Such trees are also very useful and underutilized tools for solving difficult problems in the social sector. They will help you identify root causes and expand and organize potential solutions.

The best way to learn how to use them is by studying examples. We'll start simple, with a profit tree for a business that sells sandwiches. Next, you will read about how option trees can be applied to two very different and challenging problems: how to improve literacy outcomes and how to save lives by preventing gun deaths.

I suggest you read this chapter in its entirety. Feel free to read quickly. While you will find a fair amount of detail in the examples, the main message you should focus on is not the *content* so much as the *structure and process*. Once you know what is involved, you can develop the first draft of your tree in a workshop or meeting with your stakeholders.

INTRODUCTION TO OPTION TREES

Trees are diagrams used to identify relationships, generate and organize ideas, and make decisions. By way of example, imagine you are running a sandwich shop and want to understand how you could make it more profitable. Working left to right, state your goal—in this case, profit. As you move to the right, break your goal into different "branches," higher-level elements that contribute to the outcome you are working to achieve.

Profit can be broken into two higher-level "branches": revenue and costs. Revenue is the amount of money you make from selling sandwiches. Costs are the amount you spend to make and sell those sandwiches. Revenue minus costs equals profit, the money left for you to keep or invest back into the sandwich shop.

Once you have this first split, do the exercise again, splitting each element into its component pieces. Revenue is made up of volume multiplied by price—how many sandwiches you sold times the price per sandwich. Costs are split into fixed and variable costs. As a reminder, fixed costs are the total amount of money you must spend no matter how many products you produce (typically things like rent and your manager's salary), and variable costs depend on how much you sell (the cost of the bread, cheese, butter, and so on).

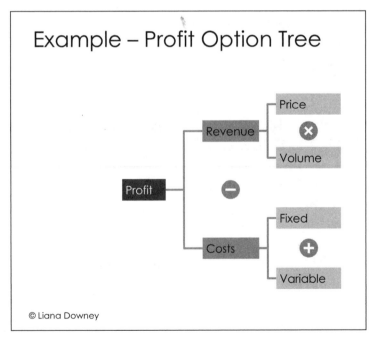

Example – Profit Option Tree

© Liana Downey

FIGURE 4.1   Sandwich Shop Profit Tree

With this layout, you can now see clearly that to increase your profits, you have two main options: you can increase revenue or decrease costs.

How can you increase revenue? This is where you start to list all your options. You can increase your revenue by raising your prices. You could also increase the number of customers—do more advertising, improve the taste of your sandwiches to drive customer referrals, open up another location, or train your staff on sales. Or you could sell more to your existing customers—offer a three-for-one deal or sell other products like drinks and snacks.

How can you lower costs? You can reduce your fixed costs by moving to a cheaper location, having your manager work part time, or paying a lower wage. You could reduce your variable costs by buying your bread in bulk, negotiating a better rate on butter, using cheaper cheese, and so on.

With this example, you can see how breaking your goal into discrete pieces can help you generate ideas. If you are a social enterprise and you rely on your activities to fund social change work, then you will want to think both about how to maximize profit, as laid out in this example, and about how to achieve your social outcomes, as laid out in the next two examples.

HOW DO OPTION TREES RELATE TO THE THEORY OF CHANGE?

You may have come across the concept of the "theory of change." Specifically, this involves laying out the inputs you get (like money, donated goods, volunteer time), detailing the activities you use these inputs for (providing meals for the hungry), and showing how they achieve meaningful short-, medium-, and long-term outcomes (reducing hunger): this is your theory for how you will achieve change.

The theory of change can be a useful approach for checking the logic of your final strategy, however it is not a good tool for *developing* a strategy. I have seen many people try laboriously to retrofit their work into a "theory of change" template, to little end. So, if you have a stakeholder who wants to know about your theory of change, wait until the end. Following the steps in this book will support you in developing a robust strategy that can then be articulated in a "theory of change" format.

OVERVIEW OF OPTION TREES IN THE SOCIAL SECTOR

Option trees can also be used effectively in the social sector to help you identify, organize, and understand much more complex problems, such as how to achieve your goal.

In the following pages you will find examples that show how to break down two quite different, but equally challenging, social-sector examples: how to improve literacy outcomes and how to saves lives by reducing the number of people killed by guns.

You may have noticed that in the profit tree example above, your branches are relatively straightforward. They are distinctive—reducing costs is an activity that is distinct from raising prices. They are also comprehensive—together they cover all the main options you have for increasing profit. This is part of the power of this approach. When I was at McKinsey & Company, we used to talk about the branches on your tree ideally being "mutually exclusive and collectively exhaustive." That means, once the branches are complete, you should have identified a series of distinct factors that impact your goal. They should not overlap with one another. And, together, they should cover all the possible options.

That works well in business examples, as you saw above. In the social sector, however, you will often find much more interaction and overlap—it can be harder to ensure all your branches are truly independent. But try. Doing so will force you to clarify your understanding of root causes and better understand which factors influence which outcomes. Do your best to keep items relatively discrete and make your list comprehensive. But if you still find lots of overlap, do not be too hard on yourself, it is just part of the complexity of social sector work.

EXAMPLE:
BE THIRD-GRADE READERS

Imagine you are running an after-school program for first graders. Like the teacher who set the goal we discussed earlier, "Be Third Graders," you have decided to focus your efforts on literacy, and set a goal for your first graders to "Be third-grade readers by the end of the year." Just as you did with the sandwich shop example, write your goal—the outcome you desire—on the left. Then identify at the highest level possible the factors that influence your desired outcome. A good split for your options here is to: increase dosage of existing programs, increase effectiveness of existing programs, and add or increase other supportive programs. Again, you should pause here to check: Have we covered all the possible factors? Is each of these factors discrete?

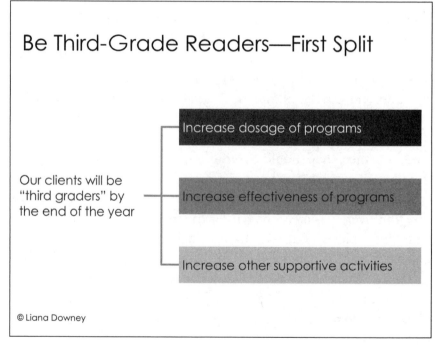

FIGURE 4.2 Be Third-Grade Readers—First Split

Once you have your split, break categories down again. What factors influence dosage (the amount of time the children are exposed to the program)? You could increase the number of hours the program runs per week—instead of children participating in the program for three hours per week, you could expose them to five hours a week. Or, you could increase the number of children who take the program—fifteen rather than four children from the class could attend.

Keep going. How can you increase effectiveness? You could: improve teacher quality; strengthen the leadership of the program; raise aspirations; or strengthen family partnerships. Or you could measure the impact of your current curriculum, technology, and pedagogy, and implement more of what works and less of what does not.

What other supportive approaches could you add? Are there factors beyond teaching that you could pursue to make a difference to the learning of the children you support, such as improving nutrition or increasing physical activity?

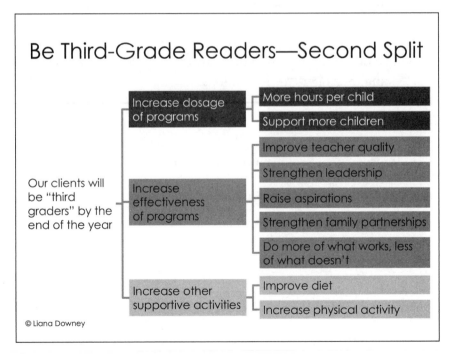

FIGURE 4.3   Be Third-Grade Readers—Second Split

Once you have outlined your factors to a reasonable level of detail, you can start to generate specific activities that you could do to influence those factors. So, what could you do to increase dosage?

- **Increase the number of hours per child**: add more funding, add more teachers, or change the scope of the program
- **Support more children**: change referral criteria, work with more partner organizations, seek more funding, etc.

What could you do to increase the effectiveness of programs?

- **Improve teacher quality:** train or coach current teachers, or recruit more effective teachers
- **Raise aspirations:** share your aspiration for children to "Be third-grader readers" with students, parents, and teachers
- **Strengthen family partnerships:** train parents on the importance of reading at home, provide access to books at home, boost parents' literacy skills, teach other strategies (picture books, audio books)
- **Do more of what works and less of what does not:** observe differences, speak to experts to identify more effective curricula, pedagogy, or technology

What could you do to increase other supportive activities?

- **Improve diet:** provide a healthy breakfast or afternoon snack, or stop offering foods that make children feel sleepier and make it harder to learn, such as soda, juice, or other sugary snacks
- **Increase physical activity:** add or increase sport or playtime, combine physical and learning activities (spelling bee races, dancing the alphabet), or include more movement breaks

As you can see, the process of getting clear on the broad range of factors initially will help you generate a comprehensive and compelling list of options for different activities. The example here is designed to show you how you can break a problem down and develop a comprehensive set of options. Note, too, that at this stage you do not need to go too deep, just make sure you've covered the broadest range of options. Later you will trim some of the branches from the tree before narrowing in on the best options, and then getting into details.

A Note on Structuring Your Tree

Getting the tree right can be hard. You may be unsure of how to split things, or there may be situations where you have multiple potential splits. Sometimes the way you split topics makes a big difference and sometimes it does not; play around to see whether the final options you generate change. If not, just pick one and go with it.

I also find that it is very helpful to create the option tree on a whiteboard (part of the reason consultants love whiteboards), because you can play around with pieces and move branches around. I assume that you will be doing this in a workshop or meeting setting, so a whiteboard allows everyone to see the draft tree. A tree is in good shape if it has a clear, logical structure, each of the pieces is discrete, and you have covered all the types of options.

Once you see a tree laid out well, it will feel right. Getting a tree that feels "obvious" is an art form, and often takes quite a lot of thinking and playing around. Do not be disheartened if you take a few attempts before you get to one that feels right.

EXAMPLE—SAVE 5000 LIVES

In this final example, imagine you have set a goal to "Save 5000 lives" (or "5000 fewer gun deaths").

I've included this grim and politically charged example for two reasons. First, if you are working in the social sector you may be dealing with similarly challenging issues on a regular basis. This example will show you how a tree format can help unpack what seems overwhelming into more manageable elements. This is a useful example of a tree applied to a goal where you are trying to prevent something from happening, like injuries, transmission of a disease, or accidents. As with the example above, before you move to specific solutions, you should identify each of the factors that must be in place for something to happen. In our example, we will look at the factors required for someone to be shot and killed by a gun, but you may also use this approach to understand what is needed for someone to contract Ebola or HIV, be injured by a drunk driver, become homeless, become addicted, become a refugee, and so on.

In this example, you could start by observing that, at the highest level, gun deaths are a factor of the number of times a shot is fired at a person and the percentage of those shots that are fatal.

Then, continue to identify branches and subcategories. As you do so, you can start to think about the kind of mathematical relationships between these factors. This can be helpful even if you are not able to pinpoint every number (and this can be very tough to do for some problems). Later, you can use it to estimate, for example, what will have more impact on the number of lives saved: a 10 percent improvement in the survival rate from a gunshot wound or a 10 percent reduction in the number of gunshots? Different branches will drive more impact than others, and you may find that a small change in one area has a big impact on your overall goal. We discuss how to analyze the numbers in more detail in chapter 5—"Identify What Works."

Continuing on, for the shot to occur, there has to be an opportunity and a reason to shoot. The number of opportunities is a function of how many guns exist, are accessible, and are loaded. Guns are fired for different reasons; some gunshots are accidental (self-inflicted or otherwise), some are suicides, and some are homicides (the killing of one person by another).[2]

Once you have a clear picture of the range of potential contributing factors, lay out what you can do to prevent each factor in a new option tree. Your hard work in identifying the underlying factors makes it much easier for you to systematically identify options

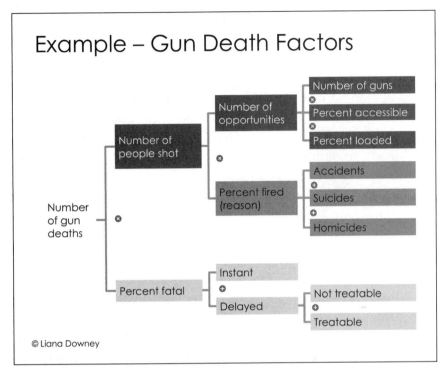

FIGURE 4.4   Factors in Gun Deaths

for achieving your goal. Below, we look at how to reduce the number of opportunities, reduce the reasons, and increase the survival rates. With an issue as multifaceted as this, you may find it helpful to break the challenge into a few different trees, as we have done below. If you feel comfortable with the approach by now, you can skip ahead to "In a Nutshell." If you want to understand what it looks like when you break a big problem down into all the options, read on!

REMOVE THE OPPORTUNITY

You could remove the opportunity by reducing the number of guns, reducing access to guns, reducing the percentage of loaded guns, and/or making it harder to fire a gun. Once you have these broad categories identified, expand each of these branches.

Reduce the total number of guns either by reducing their supply or by reducing demand for guns.

> ➤ *You could reduce supply* by limiting distribution. Today, guns are freely available in the U.S. from one of the more than 120,000 licensed gun dealers, including major chain stores like Walmart, online dealers, and the many gun fairs held throughout the country. So you could reduce the number of situations in which people can purchase a gun, for example by making it illegal to buy and sell secondhand guns, hold gun fairs, or sell guns online. You could restrict the number of retailers. You could restrict manufacturing, limiting the number and types of guns that different firms can make. Finally, you could simply make gun ownership illegal, as has been done in Japan, Australia, and other countries. You could clamp down on black-market sales, increasing policing and sentencing. Note that without doing all the math, you can see that each of these options has dramatically different impacts and payouts in terms of the total number of weapons available, which would factor into your ultimate decision about which activities to prioritize.

> ➤ *To reduce demand,* you could make gun ownership less appealing by increasing awareness about the dangers of having a gun in the home (including risk of child injury and suicide), communicating the research that owning a gun puts you more at risk than not owning one. You could take out the influence of advertising by prohibiting advertising and marketing (as has been done in other countries with other substances that can put lives at risk depending on use— alcohol, tobacco, and prescription drugs). You could make guns harder to get by increasing the cost of guns (setting a minimum price floor) or by increasing taxes, as has been done in the case of alcohol and cigarettes (and a recent Seattle gun-violence tax).[3] You could set a yearly or lifetime limit on the number of guns per person, or restrict the kinds of guns a person can own. You could increase the barriers for

purchasing guns by increasing the minimum age to purchase, increasing the number and strength of background checks, or requiring substantial training.

Reduce the number of guns that are easily accessible—you could improve technology and storage mechanisms as part of gun design, requiring a second device to start firearms, which is stored away from the gun itself, in the same way cars require keys to start them. You could strengthen storage laws across the country, requiring all guns in the home to be stored and locked, or you could ensure better compliance with existing storage laws. You could limit the situations in which guns are accessible by educating gun owners about the risks of accessibility, and encourage people to discuss gun storage openly (for example, when setting up playdates for children). You can also prohibit use in certain situations (banning smoking in public places has had a big impact on smoking cessation)—banning guns in home day-care settings, airports, schools, shopping malls, and movie theaters, for example.[4]

Reduce the number of loaded guns—to do this, manufacturers could be required to introduce technology that makes it impossible to store a loaded gun. Or, you could have an alarm or danger signal that clearly indicates that the gun is loaded and at risk, in the same way trucks make a noise to show they are backing up. You could also look at ways to reduce the quantity of ammunition available (limit per person sales, tax ammunition, etc.). You could mandate that ammunition be stored separately (as is the case in Switzerland, where men form a citizen army and are required to have a weapon but government ammunition is stored separately and centrally).[5]

ADDRESS REASONS

After looking at reducing opportunity, you can look at reducing *reasons*, both accidental and deliberate. As you are working through your own example, continue to review each factor and

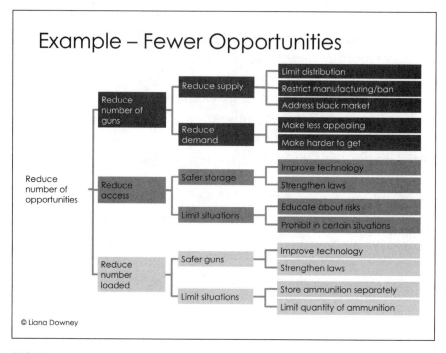

FIGURE 4.5   Fewer Opportunities

think of ways you could address each, building out the branches of your option tree. If you feel comfortable with the approach, feel free to skip ahead to the section "What Could Prevent You from Being Effective?"

Reduce the number of situations in which accidents occur. Accidents are a function both of how many times guns are handled, and the percentage of times those handling them do not understand the risks. Accidents can occur when someone is cleaning a gun, thinks a gun is fake (especially a risk with children), misfires, or does not know it is loaded. Recently, a nineteen-year-old shot himself while taking a selfie with a loaded gun, thinking it unloaded.

Each year in the U.S., more than twenty thousand firearms accidents involve children and young people,[6] and three a day involve children under the age of fifteen.[7] Thus, you could ensure that guns and children rarely have an opportunity to be together. You could undertake education of parents and children about the risks of having guns in the home; raise awareness about the incidents in which children have died; educate parents and children about the risks of touching, playing with, or using guns; encourage conversations about gun storage among parents (you may not have a gun in the home, but your child's friend might), and require mandatory training. You could also increase penalties for allowing children to have access to guns (a strategy proven to reduce accidental gun deaths in the U.S.), in the same way adults who put children's lives at risk by not having them in an approved child car seat or who drive under the influence of drugs or alcohol are penalized.[8]

For accidents that involve adults, you could strongly regulate the use of drugs, alcohol, and guns (prohibiting use or carrying of guns when under the influence, as with cars), and provide education campaigns about the risks. You could hold gun owners, sellers, or manufacturers responsible for accidents by suing or fining manufacturers or sellers for weapons used in accidental deaths and injuries (as has been done with cigarettes, pharmaceuticals, manufacturers of faulty cars, and so on).

Accidents could also be reduced by taking steps like those described earlier to make it obvious when a gun is loaded, and/or to reduce the chances of having an accessible loaded gun in the home.[9]

Preventing suicides. In the U.S., firearms are the instrument of death in more than 60 percent of all suicides. Having a gun on hand dramatically increases the chance that a person will die from the suicide attempt, with typically a very small window to save someone's life.[10] Most people assume that people who want to commit suicide will find a way, and that the means are irrelevant.[11] However, researchers have consistently demonstrated that the vast majority of suicide attempts are spontaneous, and people who survive them go on to live for many years. Removing the opportunity saves lives.[12] This was shown to be true in the United Kingdom with changes to gas ovens, it was shown in the multiple countries with notorious "jump sites," and has been shown to be true in the case of guns as well.[13]

Thus, many of the steps we discussed earlier to make it harder to access a gun are also relevant for preventing suicides.[14] Additional strategies include educating sellers about how to avoid selling or renting a firearm to a suicidal customer, and encouraging gun stores and firing ranges to display and distribute suicide prevention materials tailored to their customers.

Other options to prevent gun suicides include better treatment of depression and mood disorders, tighter alcohol controls, and responsible media reporting of suicides.[15]

Preventing homicides. When it comes to homicide, in the U.S., a growing (and highly reported) number of homicides are committed by individuals with mental health problems committing mass murder in public settings like places of worship, movie theaters, and schools. However, while highly distressing and despite the rising number, these remain a minority of gun homicides. The majority of homicides are related to domestic violence, crime, or (presumed) gang violence. This means that the strategies that will save the most lives will address a number of these factors, and not just focus on mass shootings.

Strategies to address domestic violence and other underlying causes of crime such as gang violence and robberies include addressing underlying social issues—isolation, lack of mentors, education, training, and access to legal employment opportunities. Providing training in conflict-avoidance strategies and putting in place other activities or deterrents could also help. For example, mothers in Chicago have come together to successfully act as a physical deterrent and to channel trauma and violence into more productive activities.[16] Even more can be done to tighten the wide range of current loopholes through which mentally ill perpetrators have been able to access guns—more reliable background checks (including improving the quality of the data on who is mentally ill and consistent sharing of data across state lines) and more education for retailers about recognizing warning signs. Another option could be to provide more effective support and treatment for individuals suffering from severe mental illnesses.[17]

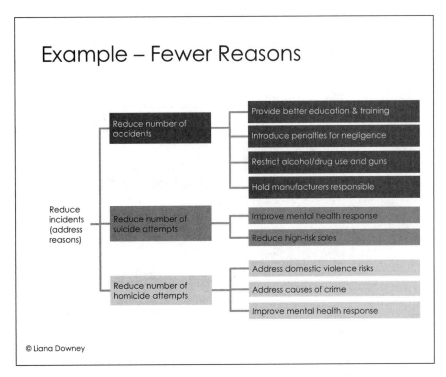

FIGURE 4. 6   Fewer Reasons

And, strategies to limit the number of accessible guns could also reduce the incidences of planned or spontaneous homicides.

INCREASE SURVIVAL RATES

Having considered options for how to reduce the number of shooting incidents, we now consider the other big branch of our tree, strategies to increase the survival rate of those who are shot.

Reduce the number of instant fatalities by equipping at-risk people with protective clothing (bulletproof vests) or by outfitting buildings appropriately (with bulletproof glass). You can also reduce the fatality rates by restricting or changing the kinds of ammunition used. For example, many police forces in other developed economies are equipped with rubber bullets or stun guns

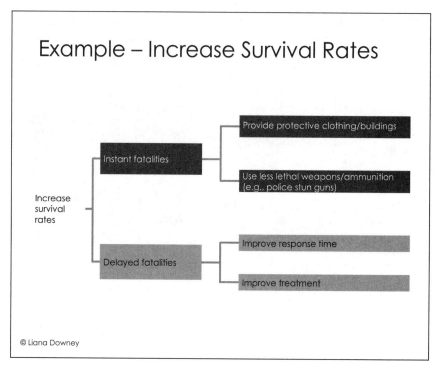

FIGURE 4.7   Increase Survival Rates

rather than loaded weapons. You could also restrict the kinds of weaponry available (handguns versus machine guns).

Reduce the number of delayed fatalities by improving medical response times (making sure an ambulance gets to the scene quickly), or by training more people to provide life-saving techniques. You could also improve medical treatment of gunshot wounds.

IDENTIFY BARRIERS
TO SUCCESS

Before you consider which of the outlined options to pursue, ask, "What may stop us from successfully implementing one of these strategies?" For example, many of the strategies for reducing gun fatalities have been attempted in the United States. What has prevented them from being successful? In most cases, one organization—the National Rifle Association (NRA)—has consistently acted to block these reforms. This is not a unique situation. Plenty of other nonprofits and governments run into one or more organizations with interests that run counter to theirs. A nonprofit trying to rehouse refugees may find political groups arguing against their acceptance into the country or city. Agencies trying to build affordable housing may run up against "not-in-my-neighborhood" groups. Groups trying to reduce obesity may find soft drink manufacturers a challenge, etc. It is always worth understanding explicitly if this is the case, and if so, why.

In the case of gun safety, the NRA is presumably also interested in supporting a reduction in deaths associated with guns. The organization supports initiatives like increased training on safety and handling of guns.[18] However, it has also spoken out about proposals from national representatives of pediatricians encouraging doctors to talk to parents about the risks of gun ownership, has moved to defund federal research into gun safety, and so on.[19] It is important to note that unlike safety training, these activities (and indeed many of the strategies we articulated) would reduce the market size and profitability of the gun industry. The NRA plays a role as a lobbying organization for what is a large and profitable industry (estimates suggest gun industry revenue is somewhere between $11 billion and $13 billion per annum, with almost $1 billion in profit).[20]

Just as with the sandwich shop in our example above, most companies and their lobbying representatives are focused on how to maximize and protect their profits. It's their job. Thus, by definition, we should expect the NRA to lobby aggressively for laws and actions that enhance the profits of gun manufacturers and against those that reduce their profits. (This is very similar to the situation in the tobacco, alcohol, and fast food industries, and so on.) Therefore, if you find yourself in a similar situation, where you have an objective you are trying to achieve but are confronted by an actor whose interests run counter to yours, think about whether you need to add an option to your tree about how to either (a) redirect those interests, (b) diminish the other party's influence, or (c) work to find areas of mutual interest to achieve your goal.

Cynics Corner

I thought we were supposed to be focusing, not adding more to the list!

It is critical that you go wide before you narrow down. In doing so, you will certainly generate ideas that you won't pursue, but by having the full range of options available to consider you may uncover something powerful that you had not contemplated before. This approach will also help you identify gaps in services, something that will be critical as we think through what you should be focusing on.

Some of these ideas sound easy on paper, but in reality they are hard to implement.

While no one said changing the world would be easy, it is important to note that some ideas are harder for some organizations to implement than others. That's a really important part of why I am encouraging you to spend time thinking about all the ideas and then, in other chapters, to identify your unique strengths as well as which ideas actually work. Of course, all of the options may be challenging, but ultimately you should prioritize those that are the easiest and most effective for you to implement.

IN A NUTSHELL

You've now seen how three very different challenges can be broken down into the full range of potential solutions. Start with your goal and identify the broad categories of options for pursuing it. Make sure each category is discrete—that it does not overlap with the others. Make sure that, taken together, the categories are comprehensive. If you are trying to prevent something from happening, like a disease or an accident, identify what needs to be in place for that to occur. Once you have done this, it will be much easier to systematically generate options for prevention. This is the time to think expansively and identify all the options you can think of. Consider whether there is an actor (or actors) whose interests run counter to your goal, and include strategies accordingly. In the next chapter you will identify which of these options is most likely to be effective and which fits best with your organization.

5

IDENTIFY WHAT WORKS

If there's one operation for a disease, you know it works.
If there are fifteen operations, you know that none of them work.[1]
—Sherwin B. Nuland

Good intentions, hard work, and intelligence are not enough to change the world. To succeed you must focus your efforts on the interventions that actually work.

Now that you have listed all the options to get to where you would like to be, you can start narrowing them down. This chapter will show you how to identify the options that have not been proven to work, so you can focus on the ones that have. You will also learn how to estimate the potential impact of each option that does work, to help you prioritize. If you learn through this process that there are no options that have been shown to work, then you should identify the most promising and build in thoughtful tracking of your impact. (See chapter 9, "Action Plan," for more details.)

Why does this matter? History is littered with stories of smart, capable leaders who jumped on the bandwagon and poured resources into programs that ultimately did not make a difference and, in some cases, did more harm than good.

I'm not going to let that happen to you! In this chapter you will find case studies highlighting common mistakes and learn three simple steps to avoid them: identify and consult with experts, review the most relevant research, and analyze your potential impact. These steps will help you make sure your efforts are the fastest path to reaching your goal.

THE CASE FOR KNOWING
WHAT WORKS

Passion is critical for success, but it's not enough. Many well-intentioned efforts to improve the world did not work or had negative unintended consequences. Examples include efforts to address heart disease by encouraging people to drink skim milk instead of whole milk, the decision to tackle breast cancer through aggressive screening programs, the introduction and rapid expansion of the penitentiary prison system, and some one-for-one models of social enterprise.

At first glance, these efforts look amazing. Campaigns to encourage people to switch to skim milk and undertake breast screening campaigns resulted in large-scale behavioral change, something notoriously difficult to achieve. The introduction of the penitentiary system marked a complete and dramatic departure from earlier prisons models, and was scaled globally. Social enterprises like TOMS have achieved massive scale and donated large quantities of necessary goods to people living in poverty.

But look deeper, and all is not as it seems. While people have dramatically increased their consumption of skim milk in lieu of whole milk, heart disease remains our number-one killer. While today more than 65 percent of women have mammograms (up from 29 percent in the 1980s), many questions are being raised about both the effectiveness and risks associated with mammograms. The widely adopted Pennsylvania model of solitary prison confinement has largely been seen as cruel and ineffective, and has fallen out of favor. And TOMS and other models, after receiving widespread criticism for their impact on poverty, have started to rethink their buy-one, give-one approach. How and why did this happen?

SKIM MILK—CORRELATION, NOT CAUSATION

In the late '70s and early '80s, policy makers were looking for ways to deal with an emerging epidemic, the high incidence and fatality rates of heart disease. Researchers had observed that saturated fats were correlated with heart disease, and early studies showed a relationship between the consumption of dairy products and heart disease.[2] At that time, most Americans regularly drank whole milk, which contains saturated fats in the form of milk cream. Policy makers decided that the easiest way to reduce heart disease and address obesity was to encourage people to switch from drinking whole milk to skim milk, and in 1985 the Department of Agriculture (USDA) definitively recommended a switch to low-fat dairy as a way of managing fat intake.[3]

By many measures this would seem to be an outstanding policy success. Consumption of whole milk per capita in the U.S. has fallen by a whopping 78 percent since 1970.[4] Americans now drink less than a quarter of a cup, down from more than a cup a day.[5] Nonprofits and governments alike had been advocating this change, and at last behavior was changing. However, the critical question is not, did the behavior change?—rather did we get the outcomes we were seeking? Did the change help them lose weight? Did people switching to skim milk experience lower rates of heart disease? Did it make them healthier?

A series of recent studies has shown that the opposite appears to be true. For a start, it does not appear to help with obesity. Children drinking skim and low-fat milk had a higher body mass than children who drank whole or 2 percent milk between the ages of two and four.[6] In adults, multiple studies suggested that "high-fat dairy consumption within typical dietary patterns is inversely associated with obesity risk."[7] It does not appear to have helped with heart disease either. A recent meta-analysis of a large number of earlier studies concluded that "based on available data, it appears that milk, cheese, and yogurt are inversely associated with cardiovascular disease risk."[8] Heart disease remains the number-one killer in America.[9]

The implications of this are twofold—correlation is not the same thing as causation, so the fact that people with heart disease have more saturated fat in their bodies does not necessarily mean that removing saturated fats from a diet will reduce heart disease. And focusing on measuring the success of an intervention, in this case celebrating the increase in the number of people drinking skim milk, may detract from the measure we should actually be tracking—are those who switched to skim milk less likely to die from heart disease than those who did not?

EASTERN STATE PENITENTIARY— THE CASE OF THE UNREFORMED PRISONER

In 1829, a brand new prison model—the very first "penitentiary"— opened in Philadelphia. A model designed to inspire true penitence among prisoners (hence the name), the Eastern State Penitentiary marked a sharp departure from earlier prison models. Historically, prisoners were housed communally behind locked doors, and abuse by guards was common. The new prison model was a complete revolution.

Instead of living in shared accommodations, prisoners were housed in individual cells. This massive shift required developing new systems we now take for granted in modern homes, including central heating and a central sewage system. The intimidating exterior was modeled after a gothic castle and belied the calmer interior, modeled on a church. With lots of natural light and high ceilings, the prison was designed as a peaceful, contemplative environment where prisoners could converse with God, reflect on their mistakes, seek penitence, and ultimately reform their ways.

A wagon wheel design cleverly enabled a small number of guards to stand at the prison's center and monitor activity in the prison wings, each of which formed one of the spokes in the wheel. Prisoners had their own small yards, and were required to wear full hoods over their faces as they took their daily exercise, to prevent interaction among prisoners and with guards.

The prison soon attracted global attention, and visitors from the farthest corners of the world came to admire the model. Fame begat fame, and replica prisons began springing up all over the world. Ultimately, more than three hundred prisons globally were based on this model. While the model obviously had many admirers, not all visitors were equally convinced of the efficacy of the approach, which was, in essence, large-scale, ongoing solitary confinement. In 1842, after a visit to the prison, Charles Dickens shared his concerns in his travel journal, *American Notes for General Circulation*:

> In its intention I am well convinced that it is a kind, humane, and meant for reformation... but I hold this slow and daily tempering with the mysteries of the brain to be immeasurably worse than any torture of the body; and because its ghastly signs and tokens are not so palpable to the eye... therefore I the more denounce it, as a secret punishment in which slumbering humanity is not roused up to stay.[10]

Dickens's instincts were right. The problem, of course, was that this concept was based on theory rather than successful practice—the hypothesis being that, given adequate time and opportunity for contemplation, a prisoner would reform his or her ways. There were no trials before the model was scaled up, nor were common causes of crime such as poverty, lack of education or job opportunities, exposure to violence, and so on taken into account. With no apparent change in the recidivism rate, an expanding prison population, and gradual evidence that what was, in effect, mass solitary confinement did more harm than good, the system ultimately fell out of favor in many parts of the world (though the U.S. still uses solitary confinement as a punishment for high-risk prisoners).[11]

So what can we learn? Once again, we see that jumping on the bandwagon without understanding whether an intervention actually works is a risky endeavor. We can also see that a promising theory should not be enough to convince you to pursue an option. And finally—we see the importance of tracking results.

BREAST CANCER SCREENING—UNINTENDED CONSEQUENCES

I suspect many of us have loved and lost people to breast cancer, a terrible disease that cuts short the lives of far too many. Survivors, loved ones, supporters, and researchers have worked tirelessly to raise awareness about breast cancer, to better understand the disease, and to do whatever it takes to tackle it. One outcome of these efforts is that doctors, nonprofits, and governments alike have routinely encouraged women to get regular mammograms, citing the importance of early detection and intervention. By most measures, this push has been hugely successful. The percentage of women aged forty to sixty-nine years old receiving screening increased from 29 percent in 1987 to an average of 67 percent between 2005 and 2010.[12] Over the same period, the number of women dying from breast cancer has declined from thirty-two women per hundred thousand to an average of twenty-two between 2005 and 2010.[13]

At first glance, this would seem to be a major success, however once you start to dig a little deeper all kinds of issues emerge. First, in the United States the rate of mammograms actually peaked in the late 1990s, yet the declines in deaths did not really start until 2003. The extraordinary drop-off has since been attributed to the dramatic decline in prescription rates for hormone replacement therapy (HRT), which began when a massive trial showed a strong link between the use of HRT in some women and increased risks of contracting deadly breast cancer, particularly amongst postmenopausal women.[14] Furthermore, the declines in death rates were not evenly distributed—white, well-educated women were vastly more likely to benefit, as they had been the group more likely to use HRT.[15]

These issues were buried for years because policy makers in most developed countries have focused on two statistics, one—the rate of screening, and two—a five-year survival rate figure.[16] A five-year survival figure sounds good, but it measures the percentage of women who live for five years after diagnosis, not the total number of women who are dying. As more screening means more diagnosis, screening alone can make this figure improve, even without a net improvement in survival rates. Furthermore, it turns out that some of the breast cancers detected through breast screening may not go on to cause harm (apparently many people have cancer cells in their body at some time, but not all of them cause problems).

These factors, as well as biases in some of the earlier research, have led a number of scientists to conclude that the effectiveness of mammography had been significantly overstated.[17] Further studies have concluded that increases in survival have more to do with improved treatments and the reduction in the use of HRT than an increase in screening.[18]

If people are living longer, then does it matter what the cause is? It does matter, because breast cancer screening is not a neutral activity. Setting aside the costs, there are substantial human impacts. A panel of specialists convened in the United Kingdom to look into the risks and benefits of breast screening recognized that there were real benefits, but raised concerns that for every 1,300 women who survive breast cancer thanks to early detection, around 4,000 women are "overdiagnosed."[19] The panel noted that, "Mammographic screening detects cancers, proven to be cancers by pathological testing, that would not have come to clinical attention in the woman's life were it not for screening—[resulting in] over-diagnosis."[20] At present, there is no clear way to distinguish these "harmless" cancers from other cancer diagnoses. Thus, thousands of women receive unnecessary invasive, expensive, life-disrupting, and life-altering treatments, including biopsies and full- and partial-mastectomies. The panel noted that determining how many cancers were being overdiagnosed was complicated, and advocated for targeted screening anyway. Research in 2012 estimated the number of women treated and overdiagnosed with breast cancers in the United States at 70,000 women per year.[21]

The debate on breast cancer screening is still unfolding, and my intention is not to discourage women who want to be tested. Each woman should discuss with her doctor what is appropriate for her, as testing can have different risks and benefits depending on one's risk profile for breast cancer. The reason I shared this example is to highlight the challenges that lie in choosing an intervention in pursuit of a goal, and to point out the importance of being vigilant throughout the implementation phase. There are at least three implications for you as a social-sector leader. First—just because something is being done by everyone does not mean it is necessarily the most effective policy. For example, alcohol consumption beyond one drink a day is known to be a substantial risk factor for breast cancer, and yet measures to reduce consumption receive much less attention and funding than screening programs.[22] Second: ask yourself what unintended consequences could arise as a result of your intervention—such as unnecessary mastectomies arising from breast cancer screening. Finally, measure the impact of an intervention (decrease in deaths from breast cancer), not how well a program is being rolled out (screening rates), and be mindful of the measures you use to calculate success (five-year survival rates were misleading, for example). In short—keep your eye on the ball, but make sure it is the right ball!

ONE-FOR-ONE—ADDRESSING SYMPTOMS, NOT CAUSES

Founder Blake Mycoskie launched TOMS Shoes after a trip to Argentina, where he became aware of the health risks to locals of going barefoot (such as contracting hookworm, a nasty parasite that can cause serious anemia and protein deficiency, and can permanently impair cognition, as well as intellectual and physical development).[23] The original TOMS shoe was modeled on traditional Argentine footwear and was sold with a promise that one pair of shoes would be donated to a needy child for every pair bought, propelling the for-profit TOMS into the public arena. By all counts, TOMS has been an outstanding marketing success, and the company reports it has given away more than forty-five million pairs of shoes.[24] Customers seem to both love the product as well as the reciprocal model and sense of direct connection that comes from their purchase helping someone in need. The company even won a prize for social innovation, selected by Andreas Widmer, cofounder of the Seven Fund, a social equity venture fund.

Unfortunately, when goods or services are provided for free, any local market that might have existed is undermined. The shoe manufacturer's product suddenly needs to compete with free goods. Economists have long understood this problem, and there are all kinds of barriers and regulations around the "dumping" of goods for just such a reason (low-cost importation that undermines another producer). Researcher Garth Frazer showed that the large-scale donation of textile goods to Africa was responsible for dramatically undermining the local textile market.[25] After criticism mounted and Widmer learned more, he changed his mind about the efficacy of the TOMS model. Reflecting on the TOMS experience, Widmer said, "I have matured to believe that following the heart to fight poverty is a terrible thing."[26]

In response to criticism, the TOMS model has been adapted substantially to address criticisms, and today many other buy-one-give-one models (such as Warby Parker, the eyeglass producer) work with more sophisticated models designed to support local job creation and training.

But how did such good intentions go awry? TOMS started with an intervention that would address a symptom of poverty (a lack of shoes and resulting diseases and injury), but did not go further to identify a broader array of possible solutions. The company did not, for example, aim to eradicate hookworm, seek to identify the deeper causes of local poverty, or systematically identify and evaluate a range of options to address poverty.

IMPLICATIONS FOR THE SOCIAL-SECTOR LEADER

I share these examples to illustrate the point that, even with the best of intentions and resources, smart leaders make policy mistakes, sometimes major ones.[27] Whether you work for a small or large organization, one that has been working on a series of campaigns and approaches for years or one that is about to launch, I hope you will take the time now to invest effort into understanding what works. In the rest of this chapter you will learn how to identify which of your potential approaches is *already* supported by scientific evidence and which approaches have been shown to have the biggest bang for your buck.

With your option tree in hand, you are going to consult expert individuals and conduct research to understand which of your options are most likely to work under what conditions, which are not likely to work, and which are as yet untested. By doing this you can start to cut branches from your tree that do not have evidence behind them. This will help ensure that you do not waste your precious time and resources chasing dead ends.

So, for example, if like one of my clients you are tackling preventable children's diseases such as pneumonia—once you have laid out all the options, you will need to understand the most successful techniques for preventing deaths from pneumonia. What would work best? Helping parents to diagnose it more accurately? Getting antibiotics to villages where they are needed? Or avoiding the colds and viruses that lead to the illness in the first place by encouraging parents to adopt preventative measures such as handwashing and breastfeeding?

While the examples above show that the issues at stake are complex, your first step is to identify and use the best-available research to inform your choices.

FIND AND SPEAK TO THE EXPERTS

To identify the relevant research, pick up the phone! Get in touch with key experts on this subject. If you do not know who to call, spend a short time online searching for books, articles, and academic papers on your subject of interest. You will probably find that a few key names keep cropping up, often those of academics who have devoted their careers to answering the questions you're grappling with. Call them. Their contact details are nearly always listed in (usually public) university address books, or you can call their departments and ask to be connected.

In all the years I have been doing this kind of research, I have always found that people are willing to discuss their work. Most academics love to be able to connect their research to practical efforts and will be happy to share their wisdom. I have interviewed experts on a dizzying array of topics over my consulting career—irritable bowel syndrome, coal seam gas extraction, back office insurance, literacy programs, juvenile justice, early childhood education interventions, obesity, you name it—and I have always had positive, incredibly helpful responses from experts.

I strongly encourage you not to e-mail. I know most of us hate picking up the phone, but having a dialogue is important for this step of the process. You want a chance to ask questions, share your full range of options, and get behind the headlines. Of course, if an e-mail address is the only contact information you have, go ahead, but try to use it to set up a phone call or face-to-face conversation. It will save you time now and in the long run. These days, since so few people call, you are much more likely to get through to the person you want to speak to. I would make sure to also get the person's e-mail or mailing address, and follow up with a thank-you note after the call.

Here's a sample script for one of these conversations:

Hi Dr. Swokowski, my name is Liana Downey. I'm the executive director of Liana Downey & Associates. We are working with a team to save five thousand lives by reducing the number of gun deaths in America. We have limited resources so we want to use only approaches that have been shown to work. We noticed that your name kept cropping up in relation to reducing gun fatalities, and that you have written some great papers on the subject. I thought *[name of article]* was particularly relevant. I would appreciate hearing your perspectives. Do you have ten minutes now to chat? You do? Great.

If you were us—which approaches would you use? Which ones seem to have the most impact? We are thinking of launching an education campaign about the risks of guns in the home, restricting gun ownership to one per person, limiting the number of retailers, or lobbying for parental penalties for having guns accessible in the home *[and so on]*. Which of those, if any, would you recommend? Do you have any advice for us about what not to do? Do you know of other organizations that are doing this well, and that we should connect with?

[Wait while you get a lot of great advice. Ask thoughtful, clarifying questions. Take lots of notes! Now, probe a bit further. You could offer to e-mail the person your option tree to discuss while still on the call.]

Are there any studies that have findings that contradict yours? Who did those? What is different about them? Do you think your findings are more sound? If so, why? Do you mind if I ask who funds your research?

Being aware of different points of view can help you avoid any potential controversies in the area you are tackling. As we've seen in the examples above, there is rarely only one point of a view on a subject. Understanding funding sources can help you understand if there are hidden agendas you should be aware of. If a researcher is not comfortable sharing her funding sources, that should set off some alarms. While academics ought to and do aim for objectivity in their research, they are often under pressure to secure funding and there is an increasing trend toward lobbyists and organizations funding research that is favorable to their interests. Also ask:

Are there any papers or books that you think are particularly helpful on this topic? *[Get the details, or ask if the person can e-mail them to you.]* Is there anyone else you suggest we talk to about this? Is it okay if mention your name when I call?

Would it be okay if we stayed in touch, as I may have more questions as we refine our approach? Thank you for your time, you've been fantastic.

REVIEW THE RESEARCH

It is a big, wide, search engine-enabled world, and a little bit of time online can get you a long way. In addition to any research that the experts you speak with suggest you track down, look for studies that sum up all the other studies (these are called meta-analyses), then read them! If you only have a little time, it can help to know that all academic studies typically have a short summary of their key findings at the front.

Feel free to divide and conquer—assign each team member just one report to read, and come together to swap what you've learned.

Remember that you are looking to identify the approaches that have a solid base of evidence demonstrating their effectiveness. Which programs have been shown to definitely improve the outcomes you are seeking to achieve, after controlling for other variables? Do not make the skim-milk mistake (believing that because fats are linked with heart disease, drinking skim milk instead of whole milk will reduce heart disease)—you need to actually know whether people who drink more skim milk get less heart disease.

Next, look for hints and clues around implementation. Was the approach proven just in a clinical setting? Has anyone actually tested this in the field? Do we know what criteria need to be in place for the approach to be successful, and is this going to be realistic for you?

Some academic papers are more accessible than others. If you find that you are getting bogged down in confidence intervals or other statistical terminology that you don't feel comfortable with, get on the phone again—call the author of the study and ask for an explanation in plain English. Would she recommend that you pursue an approach similar to her own? Is it more likely to work than another approach? Alternatively, consider reaching out to umbrella organizations (like those you identified in chapter 2, "Get the Facts") to ask for their current interpretation of the research and their recommendations as to which options are relevant and worth pursuing, and which are not worth pursuing.

If you have ideas that are not backed by evidence, cross them off your list. You don't want to pursue them. Go for what works. If you really want to try something that has never been done before, then understand that the barrier for funding will be higher and you had better track your results.

Focus on outcomes, not inputs. If you're interested in preventing people from dying from a disease, increasing literacy, increasing participation in the arts, or reducing drug addiction, to name a few examples, then make sure that the approaches you are advocating are effective; make sure that they are actually saving lives, helping people learn to read, bringing art to a wider audience, and resulting in fewer drug addictions. If you are not sure, but decide to go ahead and implement an approach anyway, then make sure you are still tracking the outcomes, not the input measure. So, for example, do not measure how many people you screen for breast cancer or how many people you provide job training to. Instead, measure the results—how many lives were saved or how many people got and held down jobs with living wages. Hopefully by now, you have a goal that is focused on an outcome, so this will be easier.

ASSESS POTENTIAL IMPACT

So, once you have removed options that do not have evidence to support them, take some time to assess which of the remaining options is likely to help you reach your goal soonest. That is, what do the numbers (if you were able to put them in) on your option tree tell you about the potential impact of each option? You may find that accurate numbers are hard to come by, especially in countries with poor infrastructure, in a highly contentious field, or in otherwise under-resourced areas. Just do the best you can, knowing that some facts and sensible estimates will always be more useful than nothing.

To see how this can play out, let us go back to our example of saving five thousand lives by reducing the number of gun deaths. Getting reliable data on gun fatalities in the U.S. is difficult, so for this example, I've pulled from a range of different sources to get the best available estimates.[28]

Recall that our goal is five thousand lives saved. Which option will get you there fastest? Let us start broadly by looking at some of the insights from the numbers. First—there are many guns in the country—estimates range between 270 million and 310 million.[29] The number of households that own a gun is going down, but the total number of guns is going up, as a smaller number of people are buying more weapons. A large number of these guns are loaded and then stored in easily accessible locations. While there is no number for all households, 55 percent of guns stored in homes with adolescents and children are accessible by them (indeed 73 percent of children know where guns are stored).[30] Assuming that households with children are more likely to exercise caution when storing guns than households without children, this figure could understate the total number of accessible guns across all households, so to be conservative, we've used the 55 percent figure. The same source estimates that 8 percent of these are stored loaded, again suggesting that the number is higher for all households.[31] There are more than one hundred thousand people who are shot and injured on average in the U.S. each year—these numbers come from statistics

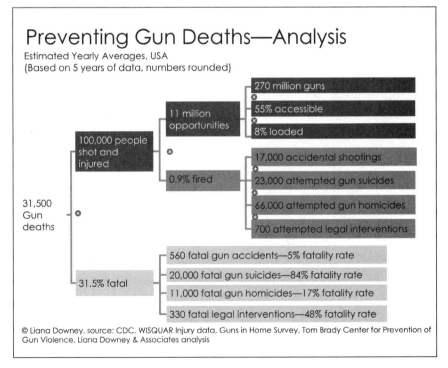

FIGURE 5.1 Reducing Gun Deaths—Analysis

reported to police or hospitals, which also probably underestimates the actual number of shots and injuries (the Center for Disease Control puts the number of nonfatal gun crime victimizations at 467,000).[32] The majority of injuries result from homicide attempts (which includes domestic violence, crimes, gang violence, and mass shootings), but slightly more fatalities come from suicide attempts, because these shots are likely to be more deadly.

Of course gun deaths are a very complex issue, with all kinds of underlying causal relationships, but even here, this high level approach can be useful prioritizing. To understand where we may be able to make a difference, let's start at the bottom of the tree and look at fatality rates, currently estimated to be just above 30 percent.[33] A 20 percent improvement in the fatality rate would seem promising, suggesting that approximately 1,800 lives would be saved, but we really need to know how many people are killed instantly and how many are not—as only a subset of those shot would benefit from a faster medical response time or better treatment.

As the 32 percent fatality rate covers a lot of variability, it makes sense to look at the next level of detail. Self-inflicted gunshots have the highest fatality rate and account for the most deaths, and because of the intent to kill and the typically isolated nature of the incident, it is likely to be difficult to increase the survival rate by improving medical response time or treatment. The same is likely to be true for homicides—typically the person shooting someone with an intent to kill is not concerned with getting the ambulance there faster, though in some situations where there are witnesses, lives could be saved if medical teams were able to respond more quickly. However, accidents are likely the option where responsiveness would predictably have the greatest impact, and these account for a very small portion of the total, with a correspondingly low fatality rate. So reducing fatality rates is probably not the most impactful option.

What about addressing the reasons behind a shooting—accidents, homicide, and suicide? Gun accidents are largely a function of the availability of a loaded gun and the percentage of people who do not understand the risk. Reducing the number of available guns will have a huge impact on the number of accidents, as will holding people more accountable (indeed in twelve states in the U.S. where such laws have been enacted, unintentional firearm deaths fell by 23 percent among children under fifteen years of age). Other options, those concerning safe storage and education about firearms, could be relevant, though not necessary if guns aren't present in the home. However, while devastating, these fatalities are a relatively small portion of the overall total, and a 20 percent drop in accidents would lead to just over a hundred lives saved.

What about if we were able to address the underlying reasons behind homicide and suicide (such as poverty and mental illness)? If we were able to reduce the incidence of attempted homicides and suicides by 20 percent, we could save almost 6,000 lives. The question then is one of feasibility. Has anyone reduced gun homicides and suicides by 20 percent without reducing access to guns?

What about reducing gun ownership? What about if we could reduce the number of households with guns by 20 percent? We know that, in fact, gun owners are not on average more suicidal or more inclined to domestic violence than others. Rather, it is the presence of the weapon that makes suicide attempts and domestic violence episodes more likely to be fatal. If there is a gun in the home, it is much more likely that someone will attempt suicide and succeed.[34] Similarly domestic violence homicides have also been shown to be linked to the presence of guns in the home, increasing the risk of death by homicide by 90 percent.[35]

If you reduce the number of people who have guns, while assuming that estimates about how many guns are stored loaded and how frequently they are accessed stay the same, then we would expect to see a reduction in suicide and domestic violence fatalities.[36] Indeed, this is what has been shown to happen in areas that restrict supply and reduce gun ownership (like New York City which has a firearm death rate less than half the national rate).[37] Let's leave for one moment the possibility that we might also see a reduction in gang violence, crimes, or even domestic violence, even though this has been the experience of other states and countries.[38] Instead, to be conservative, let's just focus on suicides, then this 20 percent reduction in the number of people with guns would result in roughly four thousand lives saved every year. [39] Thus any approach that works to reduce household gun ownership will have a significant impact in helping us reach our target of five thousand fewer gun-related deaths.

So, you've narrowed the field. The shortlist of high impact options is to a) tackle the causes of suicides or homicides or b) reduce the number of households with guns. Your next step would be to go back to your expert research, and determine whether mental health strategies or gun control strategies have proven most successful in other situations (in general gun control has proven easier and more impactful). You consider, as per the next chapter, which of these options your organization is best placed to pursue.

This type of analysis, combined with insights about what works from research and interviews, will help you hone in on the most impactful strategies.

SUMMARIZE AND SHARE YOUR FINDINGS

You will be reviewing the results of this research with your broader decision-making group in your final workshop. To ensure that people come to that meeting prepared, spend some time capturing the findings from your research and analysis, and put it in one or two slides. Send these around to your decision makers before the workshop. It may also make sense to circulate the most relevant article or articles on the subject.

Cynics Corner

We don't have the time or funding to commission a literature review; what should I do?

If you do not have the resources to commission a literature review—that's actually a good thing! It is better not to outsource this work.

It is a very different thing to read material yourself than to have someone else tell you what she learned. If you want to be a leader in your field, then you need to commit to keeping yourself up to speed. Besides, taking the time to get to know relevant experts, ask thoughtful questions, and understand the nuances will save you a lot of time later on, because you will learn from others' mistakes and focus your energy in areas that work.

Of course you are busy, which is precisely why I am not suggesting you try to read every document that has been produced on the subject. Go for the critical documents. If you are not sure which ones matter most, ask the experts and/or review the meta-analyses.

How do I know the "experts" actually know what they're talking about?

It can be tough to know if you have found the right experts. We've already seen from some of the examples above that research is complicated. In the real world, people make mistakes in their study methodology, have biases they are not aware of, may be funded by someone with an agenda, and, sadly, may even make up their study results (it is rare, but it does happen). All you can do is use your wits, ask smart questions, get the information, and listen to your instincts. Ultimately, you will make a decision and track your results. That way, even if you have been given poor guidance, you will not go down the wrong path forever; instead, you will be able to change tactics and correct your course.

IN A NUTSHELL

Not all interventions are created equal. Spending time now to think through the options that are most likely to help you achieve your goal will help you save time, money, and possibly lives. Rather than jump on the bandwagon, you now know how important it is to take time to find out what really works.

By consulting with experts and availing yourself of the latest research, you will be able to identify which options work and which don't. By the potential impact of different options, you will also be able to gauge whether some options are likely to get you to your goal sooner than others. This research and analysis work will be used in your final workshop to help you prioritize your activities.

6

IDENTIFY YOUR STRENGTHS

But of course we can't take any credit for our talents.
It's how we use them that counts.
—Madeleine L'Engle, *A Wrinkle in Time*

Now it's time to spend a little bit of time looking inward. In this chapter you will take a good hard look at your organization to identify your distinctive talents and capacity. You will then use this information to help you focus your efforts on the activities you are uniquely placed to pursue.

This is different from the SWOT (strengths, weakness, opportunities, and threats) exercise you may have come across before. The SWOT is a favorite exercise in nonprofit planning sessions, but it is often a big time waster. In a typical SWOT analysis, the answers go up on a whiteboard or flip chart and stay there. The answers are rarely used to make decisions. You're busy! Therefore, you should only spend time on activities that are going to change what you do and help you increase impact. Instead of generating a lot of answers you will not act on, you will identify your assets and capabilities and use those to help decide which option you should pursue.

You may be relieved to hear that you do not need to do more research; this process simply requires you to think. It is best done in a workshop setting (see sidebar for more details), where you will work through the exercises in the remaining chapters. This second workshop will probably require five or more hours in total. It is a long meeting but you will cover a huge amount of ground, and you will be finished with the Mission Control process at the end of it. I suggest you read each of the remaining chapters before you hold your workshop.

In the second workshop, make sure to include your decision makers and a diverse mix of people who represent different perspectives and vantage points but know your organization well. You may want to include your top team, a client or someone who cares

---

Suggested Agenda for Workshop 2

In your first workshop, you revised your facts, set your goal, and identified the full range of options. You then spent time researching which of your options is most likely to work.

In the second and final workshop you will identify your distinctive strengths, make choices, tell your story, and develop an action plan. Set aside a half to three-quarters of a day.

A suggested agenda for this workshop is as follows:

- Introductions and overview of objectives (15 minutes)
- Discuss desirable behavior for workshop (5 minutes)
- Assess impact
  - Review findings from research and analysis (chapter 5) about what works (30–40 minutes)
  - Discuss implications for your choice of options (15 minutes)
  - Rate impact (15 minutes)
- *Break*
- Assess fit
  - **Identify organizational assets and capabilities (30–45 minutes) (*Focus of this chapter*)**
  - Discuss implications for your choice of options (15 minutes)
  - Rate fit (15 minutes)
- Choose your approach (30–45 minutes)
- Discuss story (30 minutes)—chapter 8
- Plan for action (30 minutes)—chapter 9

---

for a client, board members, and possibly an important funder or partner. If you do this, be sure you are clear about who gets to make decisions—for example, you may seek input from everyone but have only a subset of those present vote on your final approach. Before the meeting, send out your agenda, your facts, and a summary of the questions discussed below. Encourage participants to read the materials and come to the meeting with their own questions and responses to get the conversation started.

You should also invite a person to the meeting to play the role of "challenger." Ideally, this person should not be an insider nor have a lot of preconceptions about your organization. Her role will be to challenge you on any claims you make about your strengths and capabilities. The less she knows about your organization, the more likely she is to keep you from falling back on firmly held beliefs that may not necessarily be true. The "challenger" does not need to be a professional facilitator. You are looking for someone intelligent, thoughtful, and willing to question your claims. Good candidates could include a colleague of a board member, a friend, or even a family member. (If you do choose a family member, just make sure to ask him to challenge you on content, not on why you borrowed a sweater without asking twenty years ago!) Make sure you explicitly ask him to test your conclusions and demand you make a compelling case for why you think you're particularly good at something, not just to take you at your word.

Once you have assembled everyone, discuss the questions that follow. You do not have to work through every single bullet point below, just make sure you cover all the broad topic areas. Before the meeting, someone may be able to narrow the list of questions down to suit the options you have left on your tree. The point of this exercise is to help you create a list of your expertise so that in the next chapter ("Choose your approach") you can make sure you are focusing on the options that you are best placed to implement. The detailed questions below are there to prompt you if you get stuck and to help you have a rich, full discussion.

As you go, someone will need to take notes where everyone can see them, keeping a narrow column down one side. During the first part of the process, you will be developing a list of your capabilities and assets, and in the second part you will be narrowing that down, which is where you'll need that second column.

CAPABILITIES—WHAT ARE YOU GREAT AT?

What are your strengths and capabilities? What are you really great at? Start with your clients' strengths, then look at the strengths of your staff, volunteers, board, and the organization as a whole.

PEOPLE—CLIENTS

A much overlooked asset in the nonprofit sector is the set of skills, capabilities, and resources that clients bring to the table. What do your clients already have that may help them (and your organization) in achieving the goal? Review and discuss the client surveys if you were able to do them, or, if representatives of your client group are in your workshop, ask them these questions directly. Programs that acknowledge and build from clients' culture, strengths, and skills are more likely to succeed.

Skills: What skills do your clients have at the moment? Consider leadership, community organization, parenting, language, and organizational skills, as well as resilience, experience with small enterprise, and the ability to navigate complex systems and bureaucracy to access funds, food, shelter, income, support, or other resources.

Culture/background: Have your clients always been in their current situation, or do they come from another background or situation that could be an asset to them or others? Are there relevant skills or cultural practices that may be important but have been undervalued or ignored in their current environment? For example, one of our clients, Children's Ground—an amazing early childhood program in Australia—uses local Aboriginal/indigenous parenting, healing, language, artistic, teaching, and nutritional approaches as a basis from which to strengthen health and educational outcomes for children. Starting from this perspective has been revolutionary, boosting community pride and dignity as well as improving outcomes.

Qualifications/work experience: What have your clients studied or worked at? For example, if your clients are people living with cancer, do some of them have relevant medical, pharmaceutical, nutritional, or pastoral experience? If you are running a food bank, do some of your clients have retail, hospitality, or cooking skills? Do not assume you know the answer to these questions. Many organizations never ask these question, so they never find out.

Network: What personal relationships do your clients have that may be of use in this process?

Other: always ask some open-ended questions. You never know what will emerge!

PEOPLE—STAFF

While you probably have a reasonable handle on what your staff members are capable of, there may be unused skills lurking in your organization, simply because no one thought to ask.

Skills: What skills do your staff have? Consider both program-specific skills and more generally applicable skills like community liaison, language, fundraising, project management, data analysis, measurement, financial management, legal, management, and policy development and delivery.

Interests: What interests do staff have outside of work? Perhaps your finance person plays an instrument and could help you strengthen your music program.

Qualifications: What academic qualifications do your staff have? Are any of them scientists, educators, data specialists, social workers, or other experts?

Culture/background: Do any of your staff have relevant shared experiences or a cultural background similar to that of your clients? For example, do you have former refugees working with newly arrived refugees, former addicts now helping those in recovery, individuals who have been incarcerated if you are working with the justice system, or staff who grew up in a community you are working with?

Work experience: Do your staff have other relevant work experience? Have they been in your organization a long time, worked for other comparable organizations, or have new ideas from working in another country, industry, or sector that they could share?

PEOPLE—VOLUNTEERS

Do you have a particularly committed, sizable, or capable group of volunteers? If so, lucky you! Volunteers are an often under-tapped resource, brought in for specific (and sometimes fairly mechanical) tasks but not always matched to the work for which they are best suited.

Skills: Are your volunteers good at what you need them to do? Do you have a sense for what they are able to do compared to what you are asking of them? If, for example, you run an animal shelter and you have weekend volunteers come in to help with grooming, is it possible that one of your volunteers is also good at designing websites, running social media campaigns, or fundraising?

Interests: What are your volunteers passionate about? People get involved with a nonprofit precisely because they want to work on something outside of their day jobs.

Culture/background: Do your volunteers understand the issues of the clients you are serving? (In some cases they may *be* the clients you are serving; many nonprofits have a kind of barter system working.)

Qualifications: What academic qualifications do your volunteers have?

Work experience: Where else have your volunteers worked? Do they volunteer with other comparable organizations? If so, do they have some suggestions about how you could improve your processes based on what they've seen work elsewhere?

How Not to Run Your Volunteer Program

As a brief aside—here's an example of how not to run your volunteer program. A few years ago, I met an impressive, charismatic, and capable woman who had owned and managed several very successful retail stores over the course of her career. She had a great understanding of inventory management and sales, and upon retiring decided she could share her skills by volunteering to work full time in a nonprofit recycled clothing store, a bit like Goodwill. Unfortunately, when she got there, she found the volunteer system was run in a very rigid hierarchy. No one ever asked her about her skills or capabilities, only whether she had worked there before. Since she hadn't, she spent three months in the back sorting bags, forbidden from stepping into the store, hanging the clothes, or handling the till. The store was not thriving. It was not arranged in an appealing way and the mechanisms they used to sort and store inventory were inefficient. Given the chance, she could have helped them tremendously. After three months of patiently sorting bags, she gently tried to share some ideas. These were quickly rebutted, as she was reminded of her place in the hierarchy by the more "experienced" staff. Finally, feeling frustrated and underappreciated, she took her skills to a "competitor" organization that was thrilled to put her to work, and saw a big impact in sales as a result.

PEOPLE—BOARD

As you did for the categories above, review skills, interests, qualifications, and capabilities. Ask your board if they feel their skills are being adequately utilized. I ask this question of boards a lot, and typically find that most people feel they have more to offer. It is also surprisingly common to find the untapped skills they have line up quite well with the unmet needs of the organization. This happens because people simply do not get around to asking the question— what are you good at, and what do you like doing? When you can create a positive cycle of board members feeling valuable and useful, they will feel more connected to your organization and be more comfortable giving of themselves and reaching out to their network.

In addition, consider skills that are specific to effectively running a nonprofit, social enterprise, or government board. While many people will be quick to ask if board members are well networked, it is important to note that the best boards are not just fundraising machines, but truly help manage the risks, strategy, and future growth and impact of the organization. So it's important that a board include a mix of skills: client (and/or carer) representation, governance, facilitation, auditing, financial management, strategy, information technology, legal, evaluation, and program skills. How does your board (if you have one) compare?

INSTITUTIONAL

What are you particularly good at doing as an organization? How are you on the following dimensions?

Client recruitment/trust: Are you particularly good at engaging clients? Do they find you a safe partner or organization to work with?

Volunteer recruitment: Are you good at rallying volunteers to help you out? Do you excel at managing them and allocating them to relevant work?

Partnerships: Are you good at building partnerships and/or maintaining partnerships with others?

Convening: Are you particularly good at bringing different organizations together to collaborate? Do people pick up the phone when you call?

Relationships: Do you have strong relationships with influential individuals (celebrities, major donors, movers and shakers)?

Fundraising: Are you great at raising in-kind donations (donated goods) or money? Are you particularly effective at raising funds through one or more kinds of donors? For example, some organizations excel at building strong relationships with a few individual donors, running great events, submitting government applications, or working with foundations.

ASSETS—WHAT DO YOU HAVE?

Now that you have identified your capabilities, think about your assets. What do you *have* that is of value, or of use?

FINANCIAL ASSETS

This is a good time to refer to the work you did earlier on your organization's financials (in chapter 2). Make sure your team understands what proportion of your costs are fixed, how much it costs you to serve a client, and (if you were able to do this analysis) how much it would cost you to serve an additional client (your marginal costs) if you were to expand.

Fundraising: Referring to the work you did in the last chapter, how much money have you raised, from which sources, and how has this changed over time? Do you need to raise more to meet your operating budget for the year? If so, how much?

Cash reserves: How much cash do you have? At your current spending rate, how long would this last you? Do you have an endowment or other source of predictable income?

Access to capital: Do you have a line of credit with a bank? Do you have, or are you able to get, a loan from a bank or other funder? Have you successfully run capital-raising campaigns in the past? Have you explored or used emerging financing instruments like social impact bonds?

PHYSICAL AND VIRTUAL ASSETS

What do you have that you can use?

Site: Do you have a hall, office space, campuses, geographic locations or a big block of land you have purchased to conserve? Do you have multiple locations close to clients or transport?

Inventory: Do you have a valuable inventory of goods (food, toys, books, etc.)?

Technology: Do you have a lot of computers, tablets, phones, servers? Do you have any interesting or proprietary software or apps?

Database: Do you have interesting, useful, or unique information about your clients and their needs and outcomes?

Curriculum: Have you developed training or a curriculum that works and is distinctive?

Library: Do you have a library or collection of important material?

PARTNERSHIPS AND NETWORKS

No organization acts alone. Take time to reflect on who you know, how you work together, and what untapped opportunities for collaboration may exist.

Access to clients: Do you have relationships with other organizations that refer clients to you?

Increased ability to deliver services: Do you have partnership arrangements that enable you to do more for your clients by pooling resources? Do you partner with other organizations to share expertise, training, consulting, or other services that may strengthen your capacity and impact? Do you share "back office" resources like accounting, human resources, or information technology? Are you part of a group that is sharing databases or information, or is tracking your collective results?

Referral partnerships: Do you refer clients to other organizations—either those clients who you cannot serve or those who have needs that are not the focus of your organization? Do you have partnerships with organizations that refer clients to you?

Funding partnerships: Do you share in-kind donations, do joint marketing of your services, or run collaborative fundraising campaigns with others?

Access to expertise: Do you partner with academics or other specialists who can help you work more efficiently and can bring you up to date on the latest thinking?

Lobbying partnerships: Do you have strong relationships with other organizations to help you lobby on behalf of your clients or for legal changes that better support your mission and work?

OTHER ASSETS

What else do you have that could be helpful in achieving your goal?

Processes, approaches, or programs: Do you have a way of doing something that is both effective and distinctive? For example, I've worked with clients who are really good at structuring successful international financing partnerships (the Nature Conservancy). I've also worked with those who have a real knack for ensuring their clients are treated with dignity, which helps their clients better identify and tap into their own strengths (Room to Grow).

Brand/reputation: Do you have a strong, well-recognized, and/or trusted brand? In the business world, if a company is acquired, their brand and/or reputation are considered to have real monetary value. In the social sector, a strong reputation can be equally valuable. It can help you raise money, form partnerships, change policies, and attract clients and resources. Are you highly regarded in the community? Do people think of you when they first think of an issue?

Other: What else do you have that is of value or use?

WHICH OF YOUR CAPABILITIES AND ASSETS ARE DISTINCTIVE?

As a team, use the questions above to generate a list of your capabilities and assets. Then, still working together in the workshop, assess whether these capabilities are actually distinctive. Are there things that *only you* can do? Understanding your unique strengths will help you identify what the world needs most from you.

Refer to your sector overview—the list of other organizations tackling challenges that are similar to yours. This will help you identify whether your listed assets and capabilities are distinctive, rather than something others also do well. This is the time for your "challenger" to push you to ensure you can back up your claims.

If you have a long list and/or a big group, consider voting. For example, if you have ten to fifteen things on your list, each person should vote for his top three. If you have more, people can vote for their top five. If you have a big group, you can do this by a show of hands as someone lists each item, or by posting the list and asking people to write their initials next to their selections.

Once participants have voted, you will probably find some areas of strong agreement. For these areas, your challenger should ensure you have evidence to support your claim. For example, if you have nominated staff experience and capacity as a distinctive strength—ask whether this was chosen because you like and respect one another? (This is a lovely but not particularly compelling reason.) Or is that selection actually based on some meaningful understanding of the staff qualifications and experience of other organizations working in your field? If you have nominated your volunteers as a distinctive asset, is this because you have more volunteers than others or because you have evidence to suggest they are actually more productive than others?

For those assets that only have a few votes, ask one of the people who voted for that area to make the case for why it is distinctive, and follow this with a debate and discussion. Typically, you will find that after this process some items can be easily selected or dismissed. After you have discussed all the items, let everyone vote again. Often, there will be more convergence. Whatever happens, tally the votes and record your highest-ranking assets and capabilities.

Cynics Corner

We only talked about strengths—what about all the things we need to work on?

You will build a stronger, more effective organization by explicitly choosing to build on your strengths. While you will need to consider risks, I suggest you do this only after you have narrowed your list down some more. This will save you time, as you will only be identifying risks for the activities you are more likely to pursue. An important part of your action plan (see chapter 9, "Plan for Action") will be ensuring you have the necessary capabilities in place to succeed.

Voting? That doesn't seem very scientific!

Voting is a pragmatic way to identify your distinctive assets and capabilities. While some of your strengths may be assessed objectively (for example, whether you have more referral partners than another organization), others (such as whether your volunteers are more committed) will require subjective judgment. Objective assessment is critical in chapter 2, "Get the Facts," and you should be as scientific as possible in choosing the strategies to help you reach your goal (chapter 5, "Identify What Works"). Choosing the right strategies could literally be a life or death decision for your clients, so getting it right matters. But for some of the choices about your strengths and capabilities, you will just have to make the best decision you can. Therefore, I suggest you get as informed as you can, have a robust discussion, and vote.

IN A NUTSHELL

Work as a team to identify your assets and capabilities. First consider your clients' strengths and capabilities, then systematically review other assets and capabilities, including staff, volunteers, boards, finances, and other physical and virtual assets and infrastructure, such as curricula or databases. Have someone challenge you once you have compiled the list to make sure that you only list the assets and capabilities that are distinctive, and that set you apart from other organizations. You will use this information in the next step to help you identify the options that best fit with your strengths.

7

CHOOSE YOUR APPROACH

One's philosophy is not best expressed in words; it is best expressed in the choices we make.[1]
—Eleanor Roosevelt

You have the facts on your clients, organization, sector, and the broader environment. You have now made two critical choices—who you should focus your energy on serving and which spine-tingling goal you will pursue. Now that you know where you are headed, it is time to choose how you will get there. You have laid out all your options. You know which of these work, which do not, and which are unproven. You know what you're good at. Now it's time to put it all together and choose the path to your goal based on what works, what you are uniquely qualified to do, and what will have the most impact.

If you are following the suggested work plan, the process of choosing which options to pursue will be done as a team in your second workshop (see sidebar for a suggested agenda). If you have decided not to use a workshop approach, then you should still endeavor to gather groups of relevant decision makers to discuss topics. You may decide that you do not need all people at all meetings, so you can read each chapter and decide who you would like involved in the work described in that chapter. Then set up a series of shorter meetings, say 1 to 2 hours per meeting, aligned with each chapter and work through the exercises as described. If you are working independently, for example, if you are in the process of starting a nonprofit, I would still encourage you to find

---

Reminder—Agenda for Workshop 2

As a reminder, the suggested agenda for the second workshop is as follows. This chapter covers the steps in bold.

A suggested agenda for this workshop is as follows:

- Introductions and overview of objectives (15 minutes)
- Discuss desirable behavior for workshop (5 minutes)
- **Assess impact**
  - Review findings from research and analysis (chapter 5) about what works (30–40 minutes)
  - Discuss implications for your choice of options (15 minutes)
  - **Rate impact (15 minutes)**
- *Break*
- **Assess fit**
  - Identify organizational assets and capabilities (30–45 minutes)—chapter 6
  - Discuss implications for your choice of options (15 minutes)
  - Rate fit (15 minutes)
- **Choose your approach (30–45 minutes)**
- Discuss story (30 minutes)—chapter 8
- Plan for action (30 minutes)—chapter 9

---

some people to work with. Just having someone to challenge and strengthen your thinking will better position you for success. If you are not sure who to reach out to, consider people working in the field already, potential clients, partners, supporters, or other trusted advisors or mentors.

IDENTIFY THE SWEET SPOT

To choose among the various options you identified in chapter 6, we will aim for the sweet spot—the intersection between the

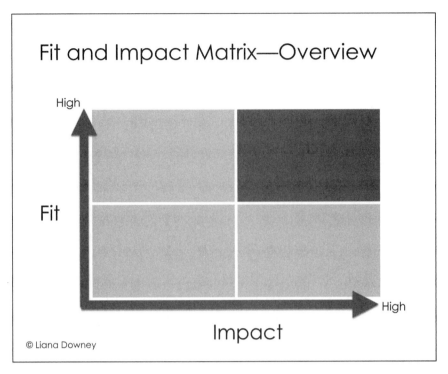

FIGURE 7.1   Fit and Impact Matrix—Overview

options that are the most likely to have impact and those that fit best with your organization. You will do this by ranking each option for impact and for fit and then plotting the various assessments on a matrix, like the one shown in Figure 7.1.

POTENTIAL IMPACT

In this step, you will assess the potential impact of each option. After you have done your introductions and set some ground rules for the workshop, your first agenda item will be to discuss and review your findings about what works and which options are likely to get you to your goal fastest. This work is discussed in chapter 5, "Identify What Works." The participants who conducted the analysis of different options, research, and expert interviews should share their findings, and you should discuss the conclusions as a group. What does the analysis show in terms of which options will drive the most impact? Which interventions work and which do not? Give everyone a chance to digest the material and ask questions, and make sure people have a good understanding of the findings and their implications.

Next, refer to the overview of other organizations working in your sectors (see chapter 2, "Get the Facts," for more details). Look to see whether any other organization in your sector is already pursuing options like the ones you are considering. If your research has identified an effective intervention but no one else working in your geography or with your particular client group is doing it, then there is a gap, and you would likely consider this option a high-impact activity. However, if another group is already doing the same work, think carefully, this may be a lower-impact activity. It may not make sense for you to duplicate the other group's efforts or launch a competitive venture. Perhaps you will achieve

Template—Rating Fit and Impact

Option	Impact (high=3, low=1)	Fit (high=3, low=1)	Comment
Option One	3	1	Cannot get funding
Option Two	3	2	
Option Three	2	3	
Option Four	3	3	Super excited about this one
Option Five	1	2	
Option Six	3	1	Great idea, but not for us

© Liana Downey

FIGURE 7.2　Template for Rating Fit and Impact of Each Option more impact by focusing elsewhere or by helping that organization expand its program.

Considering both the options that have the potential to work and the gaps that exist, ask everyone present to rate each option from a scale of one to three, with one representing low impact and three representing high impact.

You can use a simple form like the one in Figure 7-2 to collect the ratings. In the next step you will rate each option for its potential fit with your organization. Later, once both impact and fit have been rated, you can add the numbers, calculate the average, and plot them on the matrix—a chart that has impact on one axis and fit on the other.

POTENTIAL FIT

Just because an option has been shown to work does not mean yours is the right organization to pursue it. In this next exercise you will rate each of the options in terms of how well it fits with your assets, skills, and capabilities, and how likely it is that you can fund the work. For each option you want to ask, "Of all the possible groups that could do this—are we the best placed?"

To assess potential fit, start by doing the work laid out in chapter 6, "Know Yourselves." Spend thirty to forty-five minutes identifying your distinctive strengths as an organization. Once you have done that, spend fifteen minutes or so discussing how that relates to the options you have in front of you. Then each person should rate how well the various options fit with your organization. Use the same rating system, one for low fit and three for high fit.

Please be honest with yourselves. I have witnessed more than one organization rush to launch an activity because it has shown promise, even if that organization is really not the best placed group to do it. For example, recognizing that mentoring was an effective way of serving clients, I saw one major charity decide to build a mentoring program from scratch. Meanwhile, just across town there was an incredibly high-impact mentoring program that was looking to expand its services. A far more effective thing for clients and donors, and a better way to reach the goals, would have been for the two organizations to partner. Your goal should not be to become the biggest nonprofit or government agency in town, it should be to make the most impact you can in the most efficient way. If you see a great idea but your skills are in different areas, partner or go where your skills lie.

Assessing Fit—Two Examples

Sandwiches—imagine you are really great at coming up with delicious sandwiches and sourcing high-quality ingredients. If so, your organization is well placed to make higher-quality sandwiches and sell them at a higher price. Thus, if one of your options was a premium-price strategy, you would rate this as a high fit (three). However, if your strength is volume—you are able to source low-cost ingredients because you sell so many sandwiches, but you are not usually super fussy about the quality—then a high-price strategy would be a low fit (one).

Third-Grade Readers—imagine the three remaining branches on your option tree are building family partnerships to improve literacy outcomes, improving nutrition, and improving teaching capacity by doing more training. If you have started working with families but have only been moderately successful, you would rate building family partnerships as medium (two). If you already provide foods of some kind and want to increase the quality, but do not have any relevant vendor relationships or staff or volunteers with nutrition expertise, you might assign this as low rating (one). If you have had significant success in training and coaching some teachers to be more successful but at low scale, and want to roll this out, then this might be rated as high (three).

MAKE YOUR CHOICES

If you are using the template from missioncontrolbook.com, then once people have done their rankings you can simply type in your data and the averages will be calculated and plotted for you. If not, you can calculate the averages manually (this is usually not terribly complicated, since we are using low numbers) and then plot them on a matrix, like the one shown earlier.

Discuss your results. Focus your attention on any items in the top right quadrant—these have the highest fit and impact, and are the ones you should prioritize. Are you happy with what this process indicates? Does anyone have concerns? Are the options sensible ones that you are excited about pursuing? Remember that averages can disguise quite divergent points of view. If, after discussing your results, some people want to change their ratings and/or you need to move things around, feel free to do so.

Typically, this process is robust enough to get you to a point where you have identified a handful of meaningful activities to help you reach your goal. If you are struggling to choose among a few that are all equally viable, then this is the time to let your hearts and passions be your guide. I do not suggest pursuing ideas on passion alone (we have seen that it does not always go well). However, by the time you get to this point, you have narrowed options to those that have been shown to work and fit well with what you are capable of. So by all means, at this point pick those that get people fired up the most.

ADDRESS THE OTHER OPTIONS

Once you have identified the options you want to focus on, you may find that there are some not on your list that line up with programs you are currently engaged in. Discuss the next steps for those you have not prioritized.

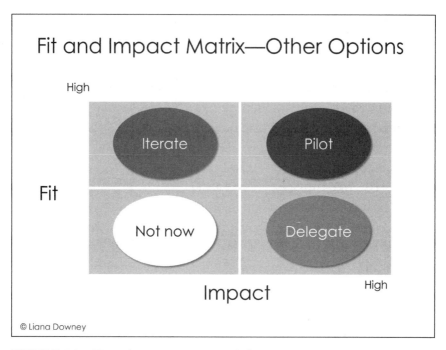

FIGURE 7.3   Fit and Impact Matrix—Other Options

You may decide to:

Delegate. If you have identified an option as having high impact but it does not fit well with your organization, consider delegating it. Is there another organization that is already doing this? If so, could you refer your clients to that group? If there is another organization not running the program but it fits well with that group's skills and capabilities, perhaps you can help them get it underway—suggest it and connect them to potential funders or other partners you may have pursued if you were to do it yourself. A good idea should not get lost, but there are many ways to make things happen; they do not involve you doing them all.

Iterate. Perhaps there is an option that fits well with your strengths but is not the highest impact of your choices. It may be that, with some more thinking, you can reimagine the idea in a way that is likely to have more impact. For example, in the way the team at TOMS adapted their buy-one, give-one model to more impactful ways of support. A helpful exercise is to ask, "What would we have to believe?" for this idea to be sufficiently impactful. Perhaps an approach needs to be proven before you take it on, perhaps you need to feel confident the funding can emerge, or maybe you need to strengthen some of your capabilities first.

For everything else, don't do it! Take the resources you have and concentrate your energy, passion, and resources into reaching your goal. Pursue the options that fit your organization, have been proven to work, and have the greatest potential for impact.

Cynics Corner

Are you telling me we may need to stop doing something we've been doing for years?

If you have gone through the process above and identified an activity that does not fit well with your strengths and is not going to help you achieve your goal, then yes, it sounds like your research and investigation have demonstrated that you may have been spinning your wheels in an activity and it is time to move on.

I do not want to gloss over the implications of such a decision. If you are thinking of shutting a program down, it may mean letting staff go or redirecting them to another activity, neither of which is an easy process. It may mean letting funding go. There will absolutely be some very difficult times in working through that process. I have seen organizations and leaders go through this process, and it is not easy, but it is worthwhile.

There are some things you can do to help ease that process, in particular to try to think about ways to hand programs over to organizations that are well placed to continue that work. If you have identified a program that is not effective, then it does not make sense for you to spend donors' money, staff time, and management attention, and to get client's hopes up, by pursuing it.

I think the activities we've chosen are great, but how will we ever get funding for them?

If you are venturing into new territory, this can be daunting. I cannot promise you that you will immediately find a funding source. I can say, however, that given where you are in the process, you have exactly the kind of organization that a funder wants to get involved with. You have a clear goal tied to a set of outcomes. You have a research-backed approach. You have thought carefully about why and how yours is the organization most suited to working in the way you are proposing. As you start to get traction, which you almost certainly will, you will find that, eventually, funders start to shape their requests based on your work.

But we are the only organization our clients trust to provide these services; if we stop providing them, our clients will miss out.

Is your organization's strength the very deep and trusting relationship you have with the communities you serve? Perhaps you are situated in a particular neighborhood or have specific religious, cultural, or linguistic ties to your clients. If so, there are some special considerations for you. This connection to community is a wonderful thing, but it often leads to expansive missions and activities, and some dilution of impact.

I know community-based organizations that provide food banks, senior services, youth services, early childhood education, arts and crafts, lecture series, sports centers, religious training, after-school programs, and more. They do this not because they have deeper expertise in running arts programs and early childhood and seniors' programs than anyone else, but because they are uniquely placed to understand and respond to their community's needs. Their focus is the community. But you should still be careful not to perpetually reinvent the wheel. Instead of building programs from scratch, consider focusing your efforts on being a conduit between the community you serve and the best available services. Identify the needs and desires of the community, connect them to the best providers you can, and track quality and impact.

IN A NUTSHELL

This step brings together all your hard work to date, so you can choose the options you will pursue to get you to your goal. At the end of this step you should have come together as a group, and reviewed the research and analysis into what works and what is likely to have the most impact. You will have used these findings to get everyone to rank the likely impact of each option. By completing the work laid out in chapter 6, "Know Yourselves," and identifying what distinguishes you as an organization. Use this honest self-assessment to help you rank the options according to how well they fit with your organization. In this chapter you have learned how to choose the options that are both high impact and high fit, and how to redirect any current programs you did not prioritize, to ensure your clients' needs are addressed as you reconfigure your work to drive impact.

8

TELL YOUR STORY

Simplicity is the ultimate sophistication.
—Clare Boothe Luce[1]

The Fenepaw River was magical. On a hot day, there was no better place to be. Winona and her brothers loved to swim in its cool, crystal clear waters. No fish ever tasted as good as the huge trout Winona's dad caught for her eighth birthday. Then the factories came. Then it was Winona's voice that caught as she talked about the Fenepaw River—cloudy, polluted, with no fish to be seen. For years she watched it die, helpless.

But today Winona has hope—she just joined Team Riverclean. At Team Riverclean we have more than hope—we have experience. We lobbied to stop factories from dumping chemicals and we cleaned up the Delta River. Now, we're cleaning up Fenepaw. We're getting close, but we won't be able to do it without you. We have three-quarters of the signatures we need to lobby against chemical dumping, and have raised $300,000 in cleanup funds, almost enough to clean up Fenepaw. If you join Team Riverclean today—that means you sign our petition, donate $60, and send the petition to ten friends—we are just weeks away from achieving our goal. You have what it takes to make magic. With your help, we will clean and protect the Fenepaw so you, your children, and their children can swim in the cool, clear waters, and maybe even catch a fish.

✳ ✳ ✳

Storytelling is critical to your ability to connect with potential clients and supporters. The aim of this chapter is to help you craft a simple story like the example above, to help you build your influence and impact.

By now, you should have chosen a spine-tingling, motivating goal based on a solid understanding of what your clients need. The goal should be simple, clear, and easy to explain. You are going to get there by pursuing only those interventions that are known to be effective and that you are well placed to deliver.

In order to ensure you have the funding, team, and resources you need to achieve your goal, you must be able to clearly articulate your story. What are you trying to achieve, for whom, why, and how will you get there? In this chapter we will discuss how to craft your own compelling narrative.

Your story has more than one audience. It is for you, as a leader, and for your team, to get you out of bed in the morning, keep you focused, and help you prioritize. It can also set high aspirations for your clients, acknowledging their strengths and creating hope for the future. It is also for your funders and supporters, the ones you have now and the many new supporters you will gain in the future. It should make your supporters feel great about their work with you—get it right, and they will tell everyone they can.

Your story is also important because, done well, it not only encourages people to support your efforts, it also helps you make decisions. We have seen that many organizations have expansive missions and lack a framework for deciding which activities are in and which are out. If a grant proposal comes their way, they may find it hard to decide whether or not to bid. If a need in the community arises, they may feel compelled to step in and fill it, regardless of whether theirs is the best organization to meet that need. This is exhausting and inefficient, requiring many small decisions every day. But by thoughtfully considering key facts and evidence, and by making active choices as a group about who to focus on, what goal to focus on, and how you will get there, you can save your team hours of effort. To maximize the benefits of your hard work, make sure your story clearly articulates the choices you have made.

WRITE YOUR STORY

You have already done most of the hard work required to write your story. Just take a moment to answer these questions:

Questions	Team Riverclean Example
Who are your clients? Can you think of a representative client?	*People who live near the river, like Winona*
What is your goal—what will you do for your clients or what change in the world are you seeking?	*Clean up Fenepaw River and restore it to its natural state*
How will you reach your goal?	*Gather signatures to lobby local government for a ban on chemical dumping; fundraise to pay for revegetation and filtration*
Why did you choose that path?	*Because we used this approach to successfully clean up the River Delta*
What obstacles stand in your way?	*Chemical pollution, insufficient signatures, and a shortage of funds*
How will someone's support help you overcome the obstacles and reach that goal?	*We will be able to submit the petition and raise enough funds to clean the river*
How will it look and feel when you have reached it?	*Magical. You'll be able to swim in the river, and maybe even catch a fish*

FIGURE 8.1 Questions to Help Tell Your Story

If you can answer those questions, you can tell your story.

TELL A GREAT STORY

Great stories are universal. They transcend language and medium. They also share some key features. They have a protagonist, goals, obstacles, and a resolution. We meet our protagonist when their world is in equilibrium, then something goes horribly wrong. The goal is to get things back in balance. Unfortunately, obstacles emerge. As the story unfolds, obstacles are overcome and the goal achieved or a lesson learned. By answering the questions above, you are creating all the building blocks of a great tale. Remember that one of the unique things about telling a story in the social sector is that you are inviting your audience to step in and play a part in your story. They have the option of bringing things to a positive, exciting resolution. You must make it clear that the happy ending is in their hands.

To make your story even more powerful—keep it simple, ensure it will help you make decisions, and keep it adaptable. It should be free of jargon, and do not—I repeat, do not—ask a committee to sign off on it!

Keep your story simple. It does not have to be poetry, but it should be elegantly simple. You want exponential growth in the number of people who hear your message, so make it as easy as possible to remember and share by keeping it under a minute. (If you are using a video format, then you can make it a little longer, but shorter is still better.) Test whether a child no more than seven years old can understand it. If you do not have children of your own, borrow a friend's or relative's (just remember to give them back)! Tell the child your story and ask him what he thinks. Take notes as he gives you some candid and potentially humorous feedback. Then ask him to tell your story in his own words to someone else. Listen closely. I guarantee you will find a way to strengthen your message.

A powerful narrative helps you make decisions. It should clearly convey what your focus is. Test it with a hypothetical or real grant proposal or project idea. Once people hear your message, do they know if you will bid on the proposal or take the project? Ask your child or your friend's child (if you have not handed them back yet). If people do not know what you would do or you get different answers, clarify your story.

A good story is adaptable. It should change to suit the storyteller and the audience. Unlike a mission statement, where the words are all lined up and debated within an inch of their lives, a story can and will vary. Should you have a version you use on your website? Of course. Does that mean everyone needs to use that exact version in every piece of communication? No. Everyone who works in your organization should, however, be able to tell a convincing version.

Your story should be free of jargon. People inevitably use buzzwords when they lack confidence in the message. Jargon only serves to isolate, confuse, and obfuscate your intent. If people are not clear on your story, they won't share it. If words like "place making," "community building," "capacity building," "social innovation," "participatory decision making," and so on are appearing in your narrative, step back and ask yourself, what do I really mean? Make choices and articulate them with confidence.

Resist the urge to have a committee sign off on your narrative! It is very tempting to try to get agreement from a committee on each word of your story. Don't—it is a fool's errand. By now you should have involved your stakeholders in making the big choices (who, what, how). They do not need to sign off on wording. I shudder to recall the long days spent trying to get the wording right on a twenty-page document for a United Nations committee. Apparently the word "safety" does not translate comfortably into multiple languages! Of course we got there in the end, and so would you, but consensus is generally achieved only at the point of exhaustion, when no one cares to argue anymore. For us, that was midnight on day four, but by then the number of pages had doubled and clarity was long gone.

If you are following the work plan and doing this step in a workshop, have one person write down the answers you listed above. Encourage everyone to develop his own take on the story. Share your versions. As you listen to one another's stories, you will probably get some really interesting ideas about phrasing or wording. People can tweak their own versions, as long as they still feel natural and comfortable telling the story. You need to agree on the key messages, but the wording can, and should, be tailored to fit the way people talk. If you are doing this without a workshop, it's even easier—just e-mail people the list, and ask them for their versions.

It can help to reflect on how telling stories works in the real world. You rarely memorize a tale word for word. You remember the key themes and tell the story in your own way. If we asked a group of people to identify key messages from a fairy tale like "The Three Little Pigs," we might hear some common themes. There are three pigs, each looking to build a home. A hungry wolf is hoping to eat one or all of the pigs. The three pigs try different building materials and learn that straw and sticks are not stable materials. Bricks emerge as the clear winner. The wolf learns to look down a chimney before climbing down. These are some key messages, and you may agree on them, but if you asked each person to tell the story, each tale would be richer and far more interesting than these basic facts. Different story-tellers will add their own oomph and power to the story. The narrative will be more engaging and authentic because each speaker is using her own words. The version I tell to my kids sounds a lot like me. Roald Dahl's version of the "Three Little Pigs" sounds like Roald Dahl. As it should. In the same way, your version of your organization's story should sound like you.

USE OPTIMISTIC LANGUAGE AND IMAGERY

Your choice of language and imagery dramatically impacts the kinds of relationships you can form with supporters. While a potential supporter may respond to an image of someone in dire need and give a one-time donation, you should be aiming for something more—a two-way long-term relationship.

Wherever possible, your tone should emphasize hope and resolution. By all means, explain the problem and highlight the need for your work, but if your audience does not take away a feeling that there is a chance for resolution, you will lose them. An organization whose dominant message is the great need in the world can end up being like that acquaintance—we'll call him Nigel—who is always complaining. Ask Nigel how his day was and he'll give you a long list of every injustice he's ever suffered. Just being with him is depressing and exhausting. In contrast, consider my ninety-five-year-old grandmother—Phyl. My Nana Phyl is candid about issues she is facing but she also chooses to be upbeat and optimistic. She gives you energy. It's fascinating to watch her in action as she makes connections everywhere she goes, and people respond to her with hope about their own challenges. As an organization, aim to be Nana Phyl, not Nigel. Strive to build a community of like-minded supporters, funders, and clients who feel they are all pulling together in the same direction. They should share optimism about your work and confidence in your ability to one day achieve your goal.

To build this hopeful, vibrant community, think carefully about the subtle signals your language and visual images convey. Every interaction you have matters, whether it is an opening speech at a fundraiser, the home page on your website, or your annual newsletter. All communication should clearly explain your goal and the needs you are addressing while creating a sense of optimism.

Use positive language when describing your clients and what you are going to do (save lives, provide homes, clean up the river, etc.). Refer to the strengths and assets your clients bring to their challenges, and what they have to offer the world. Talk about those strengths often, to your clients and to your current and potential supporters. Ensure that the dignity of your clients is upheld in all that you do. To give you an example of how this can work in practice, let us compare two similar images of girls living in poverty.

FIGURE 8.2   Sad Imagery

In the image in Figure 8.2, you see need, sadness, and poverty. This is a powerful image, and it may spark a sense of need or urgency in people. What it does not do is point to a path or resolution. It does not necessarily speak to that girl's strength or resilience, and as a result does not convey hope.

FIGURE 8.3   Uplifting Imagery

This image—also of a young girl living in impoverished circumstances—while similar, conveys a very different emotion. It is uplifting, portraying a sense of strength and optimism. This is the kind of message you want most of your work to focus on. Most people want to be a part of the positive change. That is what I mean by a two-way relationship. Supporters and donors get something in return for their donations or volunteering—the satisfaction of helping. By supporting you, people can contribute to making the world a better place. Let them feel excited by their involvement with your organization and what it may mean for the world.

Your language also matters. You may believe (as I do) that the vast majority of people facing hardship are unlucky victims of circumstance, many from the moment they are born. However, if you want to rally people to your cause you need to be careful with your language. Unfortunately, for a large number of people words like poverty are linked inexorably to personal flaws (see sidebar). In order to reach the largest number of potential supporters, you may find that language that emphasizes the strengths, aspirations, and effort of your clients is more universally appealing. A subtle shift in language and imagery away from terms like poverty and hardship toward language that draws attention to the incredible effort and determination that you know your clients exhibit on a regular basis can widen your base of potential support and the appeal of your work.

What Do You Think Causes Poverty, and Why Does It Matter?

If you are working in the human services sector, in addition to being positive in your imagery and language, you may also need to choose your words carefully. Words like "poor," "poverty," and even "hungry" have been shown to be surprisingly loaded for some people. To ensure you connect with the widest group of potential donors, it is important to understand why, and to be thoughtful about your language.

One of the most dramatic societal shifts over the last century has been the degree to which people are held accountable for their circumstance in life. Once it was not only accepted but expected that all would follow in the footsteps of their forefathers, be they peasants, farmers, or aristocrats. Peasants may not have enjoyed their lot in life, but they were not blamed for it either. However, in the last half of the twenty-first century leading thinkers embraced and demanded a more meritocratic model. Equality of opportunity was seen as the key to freeing untapped potential and enabling all citizens to break free from the accidents of birth and find their rightful place in society.

With free public education and with universities opening up to merit-based application systems, social mobility became both possible and expected. However, as meritocracy became more prevalent and entrenched, so did the "dark side" of this worldview, as Alain de Botton notes in *Status Anxiety*: "If the successful merited their success, it necessarily followed that the failures had to merit their failure. In a meritocratic age, justice appeared to enter into the distribution of poverty as well as wealth. Low status came to seem not merely regrettable, but also *deserved*."[2] As people held others accountable for their poverty, so too were they likely to consider that "it was unnecessary and possibly wrong to offer welfare to the poor...as political action to assist the lower classes only rewarded failure."[3] I mention this because these attitudes have implications for policy, funding, and the social sector more broadly.

In reality, the heyday of true social mobility has been brief, particularly in the U.S., but these attitudes remain. There have been years of dramatic change in the equality of opportunity provided—highly variable public education and years of limited access to health care, a rapid rise in extreme inequality (in 2014 the eighty richest people on the planet held $1.9 trillion in assets, the same wealth the poorest 3.5 billion people held, and the top 1 percent of wealth holders have increased their share of wealth from 44 percent to 48 percent since 2010[4]), and a highly variable track record on social mobility.[5]

Despite this reality, American belief in meritocracy remains high compared with other developed economies. More people in the U.S. than in any of the twenty-seven nations surveyed—(60 percent) agreed that "people are rewarded for their intelligence and skill."[6] Forty-four percent of all Americans (and 60 percent of Republicans) still believe that the cause of poverty is "people not doing enough."[7] A 2003 survey also found that most people in the U.S. believe that people are poor because of their own deficiencies rather than inequitable access to services.[8] Given the negative stereotypes that many people associate with terms such as poverty and the like, if you are working in the human services sector, think carefully about your language as you seek to create connection with potential supporters.

Once you have created your story using a suitably uplifting tone and imagery, keep thinking about how to make your pitch more compelling. Ask people for feedback when you explain what you are doing. Did it make sense? What do they understand from that? People are often happy to help you sharpen your message and are flattered to be asked. Use every opportunity to test and refine your message.

PREPARE A PROSPECTUS OR BUSINESS PLAN

In addition to your story or pitch, you will find there are times when you need more information to back up a request for support or partnership. The hard work you put into getting the facts and putting them into a compelling presentation for your team should form the basis of a prospectus or business plan. Make sure you put your main messages at the beginning and support your choices with the facts you gathered. A structure with a page or two for each topic could go something like this: these are our clients; this is what they want, where they live, and so on; there are no services like ours today; we are particularly good at x, y, and z, and so on. Demonstrate the evidence behind your choices. As you do this, the same guidelines as outlined above apply. Focus on optimism, and keep your language simple and meaningful. Use one message per slide. Ensure that there is a logical flow of the slides or images you are sharing.

Don't forget to ask for what you need! If you are approaching a funder, always make sure you have a clearly articulated request. Having been on the other side of such requests, I can tell you there is nothing more confusing than someone you think is asking you for something but never gets around to it. It is hard to say yes if you are not sure what the question is. (Did he want me to donate money to his organization or is he asking me on a date?) If the person says no, ask him if there is another way he can help. (I understand you are not interested in donating [or dating], but do you have a friend who might be?)

Cynics Corner

But I'm no good with words.

As long as you can convey the broad pieces of information like your goal, what you are doing to achieve it, and why you are uniquely qualified to do so, then having poetic language is not critical. Enthusiasm and belief are. However, if you are truly insecure about your ability to do this well, ask others to help you with the process. Ironically, it is often children or nonnative speakers who can be of most use here, as they are often adept at using simple language to convey complicated concepts.

I know you said keep it short, but we really need more time to tell our story.

If you feel you need to say more, then think about who needs to hear what. My main concern is that you do not go through this process and come up with a long, jargon-laden mission statement. Doing so will not help or inspire you or your team of potential supporters. Of course, different audiences will need more or less context. It is perfectly reasonable, especially in an introductory conversation with a potential funder, to provide more context about your history, some of the changes you have made, who else is involved, and so on. Many organizations are also creating and sharing short videos (the best are 3 to 6 minutes in length) on social media as a way to spread their message. In addition to your short story, it may be very compelling for a funder to hear that you used to try to do everything for everyone, but you have now made a decision to focus your energy where you see the biggest gaps and where you are uniquely positioned to succeed.

IN A NUTSHELL

In each new conversation with a potential supporter, client, or partner you should say where you are going, how you will get there, and why you believe your chosen path is the most direct route. Your message should be uplifting, clear, and simple. All your staff and supporters should feel comfortable sharing a version of your story in their own words. As appropriate, enhance your message with crisply presented facts and be confident and clear as you ask for what you need to succeed.

9

PLAN FOR ACTION

Nothing will work unless you do.
—Maya Angelou

I am easily distracted. While I believe in the power of focus, it does not come naturally. There are lots of things I am passionate about, interested in, and want to do, and that can make it challenging for me to knuckle down and really pursue a goal. For years I convinced myself that this was a strength—I was well rounded and curious, what's not to love? But over time I have learned there's a time for thinking expansively, and there's a time for focus. Big, exciting things are achieved when resources are concentrated.

Because focus does not come naturally, I have learned a number of tricks to summon it. Some I have already alluded to throughout the book—the importance of defining your goal in terms of the outcomes, tracking and celebrating progress, and having joint accountability for a goal. But there is one more secret I want to share. Sure, you can dream big and think long term—but if you want to focus, plan for the short term. What you plan to do in three years' time is nowhere near as important as what you do *today* to achieve your goal. Emphasizing the immediate future is the best way to build momentum and energy around a goal, and bring focus to your efforts.

In this chapter you will learn how to quickly put together a plan for action. A critical part of planning is expecting the unexpected. So your first step should be to reflect on the risks you may face and how to mitigate them.

ADDRESS RISKS

There are three types of risk you should account for in your planning process. The first I'll call generic nonprofit risk, the second is activity risk, and the third focus risk.

GENERIC NONPROFIT RISK

Risks that all nonprofits, governments, and social enterprises face include losing key employees and their knowledge and relationships, problems with partnerships, funding sources drying up, fraud and financial mismanagement, and failure to comply with relevant laws. There are many things that can, and do, go wrong in the daily course of managing any enterprise. If you do not have robust governance structures, clear role descriptions, a good auditing process, access to sage legal advice, and so on, now is the time to make sure you have a plan for putting those pieces in place. It is difficult to change the world under any circumstances, but if you have a shaky organization it is even more difficult. The good news is that the clarity you have created through this process will make all these things immensely easier.

ACTIVITY RISK

What are the potential risks of any activity you are undertaking? What could go wrong? What are potential unintended consequences? Remember the Eastern State Penitentiary model, which aimed for a peaceful, contemplative state to induce penitence in prisoners? The unintended consequence of their approach (now known as solitary confinement) was to drive people insane. What could negatively impact your clients or your reputation? Consider all the possible issues and make sure you have a plan to address them. In particular, make sure that throughout your planning process you build in measurement and review, to observe what is and what is not working and ameliorate any unintended consequences.

FOCUS RISK

What I'm terming "focus risks" are those that can, and do, emerge when an organization is truly focused on a goal. While I am clearly a huge advocate of the importance and impact of focus, I am not blind to some of the challenges that it can raise, and nor should you be. In the *Harvard Business Review* article "Goals Gone Wild," the authors highlighted several risks associated with goals.[1] The first risk will not be a problem for you anymore. It is the risk of having too many goals—people just can't split their focus, so you must choose just one goal. By this point, you should well and truly have mitigated that risk!

However, the authors also noted one potential issue of particular relevance for organizations with a very focused approach. Sometimes strong adherence to a goal can lead to a rise in unethical behavior. As people do whatever it takes to achieve a goal, they can lose sight of critical personal or organizational values. This may mean, for example, fudging data to be able to show progress toward a goal or, of greater concern, doing something that undermines the integrity of your relationship with clients or your impact. The good news is that this risk can be ameliorated, particularly if you are aware of it from the beginning.

Years ago, when I was helping launch a crime reduction program, the senior police commissioner said, if we focus on assault rates we'll see other crimes go up. He did not just mean that the focus on one activity might lead to a reduction in services in other areas; he meant that police officers, knowing that they are being measured on one area, may be motivated to code crimes differently. Indeed, we found evidence of how this had happened before, when there had been a focus on attending to alcohol-related domestic violence assaults. Over time, the results seemed to be positive, but the reality was different. We discovered that the computer coding would say no alcohol was involved, but the handwritten notes associated with the incidents would tell a different story, that the perpetrator had been drinking, etc. This was partly because of the goal but also because of the systems; if the officers included "alcohol" on the computer code, they were required to spend another ten to fifteen minutes entering data, which was time they could not spare. We were able to solve this both by monitoring the total assault rate and simplifying the coding requirements.

More generally, there are three ways to deal with focus risk. First, anticipate it. People are human; they want to do well, they want to hit the ball out of the park, and they are tempted to make it work any way they can. So, do not tie people's rewards to how well they are progressing toward the goal. Track the goal but reward effort. Second, measure adjunct areas. When the goal was crime reduction, we tracked not just the measure we were hoping to move but related measures too, to ensure there weren't unwanted spill-over effects, either in the number of incidents or in the way they were being recorded. And finally—track quality, not just quantity. It is not enough to house people, you want to make sure they stay housed and that the houses are fit for habitation. If children are losing weight in your anti-obesity program but are malnourished at the end of the program, you have not succeeded. If you are doing job placement but people cannot live on the wages of the jobs they get, the program has not been successful, and so on.

PLAN FOR ACTION

The best plans are ones that everyone can see and that are easy to understand. I like using a simple table that has activities and people's names on the left, dates across the top, and activities lined up below, a format known as a Gantt chart. This format has some powerful benefits. First, it allows you to get a sense for how elements of the project depend on one another, and makes sure you have planned for that. Second, it allows you to look at different people's workloads at different times and make sure no one is shouldering a disproportionate share of the burden. Third, it encourages you to think about the main types of work that need to get done. I have received and given training in all kinds of planning systems over the years, but this is still the best method I have

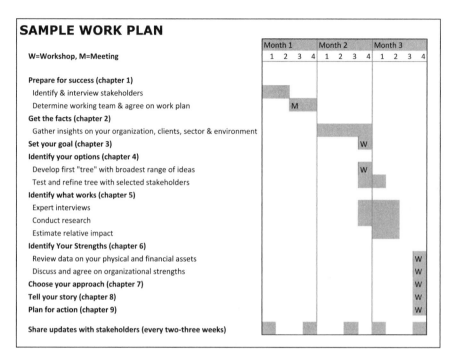

FIGURE 9.1 Gantt Chart and Mission Control Work Plan

ever come across. I use charts like these for all the projects I run—professional and personal. I even have one on the wall right behind me that I have used to help me write this book. It is also, you may recall, the format used for the Mission Control work plan, included here to refresh your memory.

In terms of the way you eventually share this document, the main thing is that people can see what is due when. If you share a work space, putting the plan on a poster on the wall is very effective. If your team mainly works remotely, then after you have completed the process below, you may want to copy it into a shared document or spreadsheet (like Google Docs). All kinds of project management software and apps exist, and one of these may be well suited to your group. However, remember that good management can be supported by technology but it does not depend on it. Go for a simple option and try not to get bogged down in or sidetracked by technology.

I suggest you plan collaboratively with the people who are going to be doing the work. You can use a whiteboard or a big sheet of paper taped to the wall or laid out on a table.

Visualize. Before you do anything else, take a moment to contemplate what success will look and feel like. How will people's lives be changed? What will that mean to them? What will it mean to you? Each of you can close your eyes in silence for a few minutes and really picture what you are aiming for. Then, open your eyes and discuss. Share what you envisioned. Some people find it helpful to draw pictures or make collages. Do whatever works for you. Add details. Make it vivid. Get excited!

Set up the chart. Then, draw up a blank Gantt chart with your timeline across the top; I like to lay out the first three months in a lot of detail, and then identify the critical accomplishments that will be needed for the next six months and year.

Identify categories of work. Next, identify the broad categories of activity. If you have decided to launch a new healthy food program to boost literacy outcomes, you might identify three streams of work—finding new nutritious foods, removing unhealthy food options, and promoting the program. These broad categories go down the left.

Identify big steps on your journey. Then, think about big steps within each of these categories. Some people refer to these as milestones—interim goals that indicate you are on track to reach your goals. For the category "find new foods," perhaps your big steps are to agree which foods, find new vendors, negotiate the relationships, and change the kitchen configuration before you finally offer the healthier options. Discuss these briefly as a group to make sure you are aligned.

Identify activities and timing. Give participants a pen and some sticky notes. Have them identify steps that need to be taken and write them down on the sticky notes. They should also write their own name, or someone else's—every task should have a person who is accountable for it. They then place the activities on the plan in the logical place. The benefit of this approach is that everyone can get involved at once and you can move things around. Alternatively, you could write ideas up on a whiteboard at the same time or have one person take notes, but that is typically slower and less energizing than having everyone write things down and share them at the same time. The benefit of the sticky note system is that people can move activities around so that they are in a logical order.

Review. After about ten to fifteen minutes of frenzied activity planning, or when you feel like you're running out of steam, step back, take a look, and see what you have. Is anything missing? If you complete the tasks outlined for the next three months, where will you be? Does anyone have too much on her plate, or not enough? Make sensible adjustments. Make sure there is something for all participants to do in the first week of the project, ideally today or tomorrow. We're aiming for action! Make sure you have also thought about how long things will take. If someone has written an action on a sticky note, but it marks the start of an action, make sure you draw a line out to record how long that activity will take. You may need to move things so they are staggered.

Tidy up. After finishing the process, it is helpful for someone to tidy the plan. It may need to be rewritten or typed up. Make sure each activity has its own line, and that it is clear who is accountable for the action.

LONGER-TERM PLANS

There will be times when you are asked to produce a longer-term plan, say a three- to five-year plan. Given that your goal may well take years, not months, to achieve, this is not an unreasonable request, and you should have a viewpoint about how you will get to your ultimate goal. However, I suggest you do not put lots of energy into a longer-term plan, simply because you should iterate your approach as you go—implement, learn, improve, and keep going. You also do not need a team to do the longer-term planning. Instead, you, or someone on your team, can draft it, then ask for people's input, as they may help you think of things that were missed. To prepare a longer-term plan, simply sit down and work backward from your goal, identifying the main pieces that will need to be in place for you to complete your goal. For example, do you need to add more staff or more sites, or need funding beyond the Plan for Action phase? If so, consider what you should be doing now to ensure you are ready when the time comes.

START MEASURING

Winston Churchill once said, "However beautiful the strategy, you should occasionally look at the results."[2] I could not agree more. Tracking your impact is essential, but many organizations still struggle with measurement. Despite substantial improvements in the social sector over the last decade, many organizations are confused about what measurement and tracking is required and assuming they need to do something complicated, do nothing. Therefore, I want to highlight the critical distinction between tracking outcomes and claiming full responsibility for those outcomes. Unless you are trying to provide the firm evidence base for a new program, *you do not need to claim full responsibility* for those outcomes. That is the domain of the experts you have been consulting. As you've seen, getting together an accurate, scientifically valid evidence base is tough. Unless you are a researcher, that is not your job. You should, however, be able to show that your approach is based in evidence and that the outcome you are seeking is being achieved for your clients.

Unfortunately, this fundamental misunderstanding causes many groups to shy away from impact measurement of any kind. "I can't fund a control group study," they say, "so I won't measure anything." No! It pains me to hear that kind of talk. If you are working to reduce the number of children dying from pneumonia in West Africa, then you have to be tracking the number of children dying from pneumonia in West Africa! If you are working to reduce chemical pollutants in a river, then you should be tracking the level of chemical pollution in that river! That is not the same thing as taking credit for every positive change in that outcome.

While this seems really obvious, a startling number of organizations don't do it, and certainly don't do before-and-after measurement of the participants in their programs. Again, let me underscore that I am not suggesting you need to be able to prove that any improvements in these outcomes are directly and wholly attributable to you. Would you even want that? If you are working to save lives, and other people are doing things that help—isn't that a good thing? But if you are not tracking that figure, and it is not improving or is getting worse (so more people are dying from pneumonia, not fewer) then you have a real problem, one that your organization must be aware of and should respond to.

If you are not tracking outcomes well, or not doing it at all, do not despair. If you've actually done the work in these chapters, you are way ahead of the game. You have a clearly articulated goal, so you now know what to track. You will be using a small number of evidence-based approaches, and will no longer be distracted by a multitude of other goals. You understand the difference between an outcome and an input. You have a relationship with experts and an understanding of the latest material in your field. You're on fire! You'll want to tell the world. Life is going to be a lot easier, and more exciting.

Cynics Corner

This sounds suspiciously easy.

This part *should* be pretty easy! People make planning into a far more laborious process than it needs to be. The really tough part of good planning is getting your facts and ensuring that your activities line up with your skills and the needs in the community. You did all of that well before you got to the action plan phase.

While writing your action plan should be fairly painless, you should still keep your wits about you. Make sure you have covered the key activities, thought about how to mitigate risks, have a sensible distribution of work across the team, and are building in time to celebrate and have some fun along the way.

IN A NUTSHELL

Keep the longer-term steps in mind, but put your energy into working out what you are going to do today, tomorrow, and over the next few months. Work together to build an action plan that reflects long-term thinking but has the greatest detail for short-term activities.

Identify the key work areas and the big things you want to achieve. Have everyone add activities and make sure every activity has someone who is accountable for it. When you've finished, make sure everyone can see the action plan every day. At the end of the first three months, you can do the more detailed process again, together or individually. To build a longer plan, include key elements that have to be in place on your journey, but do not get too detailed. Make sure all participants have something to get started on the minute they walk out of your meeting and that every activity has a name attached to it. Consider and plan for a variety of risks. Ensure you are in compliance with appropriate laws, have a good governance structure, consider and monitor for unintended consequences of your activities, and are careful that you do not push people so hard toward a goal that they lose sight of the clients or their personal values.

It's okay to make mistakes, but it's not okay to go on making mistakes because you are not checking whether the work you are doing is effective. Start tracking impact from the moment you kick your project off. You have to track what's happening to your outcomes, even if they are long term. If you do not do that, you will struggle to get and maintain momentum, and you won't know if your efforts are successful. You should also track adjunct measures and measure of quality.

Through this process you have developed your strategy, a plan to take you where you want to go. A good strategy should address what activities you will do, where, for whom, and why. A powerful strategy is easy to understand and easy to explain. It makes sense. Your team, your board, and your clients understand and can explain it easily. It reflects your context—how you started, what you're good at, and what motivates you. It uses approaches that have been shown to work and it helps you raise money. But most importantly, it has a focus—*it defines what you do and do not do.*

Congratulations! You have worked hard. You have approached your challenge with rigor, integrity, and thoughtful consideration. You have set a spine-tingling goal, and are prioritizing the options most likely to get you there. You can tell your story in a personal, engaging way, and have a crisp action plan. Everyone has something they will do tomorrow. You are ready to change the world!

Please tell me how you are doing! My team and I would love to hear about your goals, your journey, and how you are changing the world—you can join the community at missioncontrolbook.com to share your story and connect with like-minded leaders. Thank you for all you are doing each and every day to make the world a better place.

APPENDIX 1
SUGGESTED AGENDA
FOR FIRST WORKSHOP

- Introductions and overview of objectives (15 minutes)
- Getting-to-know-you exercise (30 minutes)
- Agree on desirable behavior for the day—e.g., put all devices away, be candid, don't interrupt others, etc. (10 minutes)
- Review and discuss your facts (30–60 minutes)
  - Clients
  - Organization
  - Sector
  - Environment
- *Break*
- Set your goal (chapter 3) (30–60 minutes)
  - Develop a short list of outcomes
  - Choose your desired outcome
  - Set boundaries
  - Choose a target
  - Set your time frame
- Identify your options (chapter 4) (60 minutes)
  - Use trees to identify key factors and options
- Confirm next meeting time and agree who will research the options that are likely to work (see chapter 5) (10 minutes)

APPENDIX 2
SUGGESTED AGENDA
FOR SECOND
WORKSHOP

- Introductions and overview of workshop objectives (15 minutes)
- Discuss desirable behavior for workshop (5 minutes)
- Assess impact
  - Review findings from research and analysis about what works (chapter 5) (30–40 minutes)
  - Discuss implications for your choice of options (15 minutes)
  - Rate impact (15 minutes)
- *Break*
- Assess fit
  - Identify organizational assets and capabilities (30–45 minutes) (chapter 6)
  - Discuss implications for your choice of options (15 minutes)
  - Rate fit (15 minutes)
- Choose your approach (30–45 minutes) (chapter 7)
- Discuss story (30 minutes) (chapter 8)
- Plan for Action (30 minutes) (chapter 9)
  - Discuss risks
  - Draw up plan (time frame, big steps, activities)
  - Review and tidy

APPENDIX 3
LIST OF VALUES

Acceptance	Curiosity	Helping	Questioning
Accuracy	Dependability	Improvement	Quality
Achievement	Devotion	Influence	Respect
Advancement	Diversity	Inner harmony	Reverence
Adventure	Economic security	Innovation	Risk
Ambition	Empathy	Integrity	Routine
Authenticity	Ethical practice	Kindness	Self-knowledge
Balance	Excellence	Knowledge	Self-respect
Beauty	Fact-based	Learning	Service
Belonging	Fairness	Loyalty	Spirituality
Calm	Family	Moderation	Stability
Candor	Fidelity	Orderliness	Structure
Caring	Fitness	Passion	Tact
Change	Flair	Peace	Teaching
Collaboration	Flexibility	Personal growth	Teamwork
Commitment	Freedom	Play	Tolerance
Community	Friendliness	Positivity	Tradition
Competence	Fun	Potential	Tranquility
Confidence	Generosity	Pragmatism	Travel
Conformity	Grace	Preservation	Trust
Contribution	Gratitude	Privacy	Wealth
Courage	Growth	Prosperity	Wisdom
Courtesy	Harmony	Purity	Wonder
Creativity	Health	Purpose	Work

© Liana Downey

See **missioncontrolbook.com** for more information

ACKNOWLEDGMENTS

Thanks to the team at Bibliomotion for your support, guidance and disciplined approach—Erika Heilman, Jill Friedlander, Jill Schoenhaut, Alicia Simons, and Shevaun Betzler.

Thank you Jules Flynn for asking if I was writing a book, and if not, why not? For David Carmel and Kirsten Axelsen Carmel for not laughing when I said I might try, for pancakes, and critical New York introductions. Thanks to those who helped me get my head around the early stages: Claire Ellis for your incredible friendship, encouragement, advice, and generosity—it simply would not have happened without you; Brettne Bloom, for your wisdom, practical advice and timely introductions; and Alex Glass for your incredibly helpful feedback in the early days.

A huge thanks to my inspirational clients, especially Roseanne Haggerty, Fran Thorn, Becky Kanis, Rasmia Kirmani Frye, Nadine Maleh, Josh Thomases, Susan Fojas, Susan Calvert, Mike O'Ryan, Ari Gorring, Michael Looker, Keith Bradby, Julie Burns, Valerie Russo, Jane Vadiveloo, Katie Leonberger, Allyson Crawford, Robyn Carter, Andrea Kopel, and Rosemary Addis—thanks for sharing your wisdom and passion. I hope some of what we learned together can help others on their respective journeys. Thank you also to Fran Barrett, Allison Sesso, Bill Ulfelder, and Lorie Slutsky for your wisdom and helping sanity-check my thinking.

Thanks to Diane Grady, Kathy Wylde, Eric Brettschneider, Jenik Radon, and Peter Goldmark for your guidance and consistent generosity with your wisdom and introductions. Thanks to John Stuckey for pushing my clarity of thought and speech over many years. Thanks to fellow McKinsey social sector junkies Les

Silverman, Jeremy Oppenheim, Charlie Taylor, Maria Blair, Tom Rippin, James Slezak, and Sri Swaminathan—keep fighting the good fight. Kathy Strahs, Doreen Oliver, Antony Bugg-Levine, Georgia Levenson Keohane, and Ben Foss—thanks for blazing the writing and/or book trail and sharing your advice about what lies ahead. Megan Golden—thanks for your generous, intelligent, and collegial partnership. Thanks to Lisca McClanachan, Zoe Hodder, Jessica Tregeagle, Eddie Gandevia, Haley Reimbold, Seth Rosen, Sherida Burns, Fiona Ward, Austin Mwangi, and the team at i-Mark, it's been a pleasure to work with you. Thank you Tina Brown Celona, for a 30-year, multi-country friendship and for your laser-sharp mind and editorial skills. To my Savor Sisters— Seema Alexander and Cheryl Marks Young for your sage advice, regular reassurance, and giving, I so appreciate it.

Thanks to my grandparents Phyl, Alex, May, and Neville, for providing the inspiration of lives well-lived. For Jason, Fiona and Ted—thanks for raspberry trifle, charades, laughs, your willingness to travel, and your enthusiasm about the book. Thanks Shelly for joining twitter! Thanks to Rie and Jack Downey and Tamae Ito for your encouragement, Aunty Barbara and Uncle Warren for unconditional and always practical support, Gary and Brownyn Tyson for your kindness, and the Nancarrows—Helen, Peter, Glynnis (Watanabe), Susan, and Felicity for the rellie-rallies laughs, love, and support, for my cousin Deborah Fairfull for being the most ridiculously supportive one-woman cheer squad one could hope for, and for leading by example in the entrepreneurial and book space, and to you and Dave for sage advice. Thanks Tanya McSweeney for our e-mails and for your friendship and inspirational strength. Thanks to the Cassons for your care and warmth.

Thanks to my extended family for laughter, love and support— Liz, Dick, Kathy, and Nora Twiss, Priscilla and John Crutcher, Priscilla Seimer, and Kathy and Randy Weibel.

Thank you to long-time gorgeous friends—Penny Brown, Lynsay Cooperwaite, Alison Burns, Penny Webb, EK Cameron, Lindsay Hubbard, Alex Lee, Bryant Jenkins, Amy Adams Littleton, Yvonne Fahy, Lynsay Cooperwaite, Jo and David Walker, Hamish and Carla Fitzsimons, Nicholas Gray, Rebecca and Michael Casson, Matt Spanjers, Simla Somtürk, Jason Biggs, Kerrie O'Brien, Kate Clement, Matt Wai-Poi, Naomi Hansar, Julie McAdoo, Naomi Black, Deva Grant, Katrina Barry, Giovanni Donaldson— for being a long-distance cheer squad and support network over many years and countries. Thank you New York friends and your partners—for good company and practical support in so many ways—you've all saved my bacon at one time or another: Nicole LaMariana, Carol Rock, Jennifer Meyer, Nicole Dreyfuss, Chen Yang, Pascale Blachez, Juliana Lung, Liz McNeill, Flavie Ospina, Cathy Riva, Suzanne Valetutti, Fumi Takeda, Claire Ianno, and Libbie Botts. Thanks to Raji Smiley, Louise and Joanne Anderson, Josephine Gaurana, and Samara Shanker, for each being a loving backbone to our family life, and for making our working life possible over the last decade.

Thank you for Rob McLean for your unfailing advocacy and guidance, I could not have asked for a more generous mentor.

Thank you to my Dad—Lloyd Downey, for being a great father, for your advice on the way, and for joining me on the consulting journey—what a pleasure it has been to work with you, the memories of our outback facilitating adventures will stay with me forever. Thank you to Mum—Lorraine Downey, for being the original super-mum, loving, present, an inspirational entrepreneur (at my age you had a tourist map, and two product lines to boot), a champion of the underdog, and for your absolute belief in me, and for wanting to hear the chapters read, even in hospital. Get well soon.

And last but, definitely not least, thank you Jamie, Asmara, and Max. You are my world. I still can't believe my luck. You make me think, you make me laugh, you make me gluten-free popovers, and I can't wait to read your books.

developed a sensible alternative, leaving many to suffer with mental illness, particularly those suffering paranoid schizophrenia, the homeless, the incarcerated, and those otherwise unsupported.

18. According to its website, "The National Rifle Association is the world's leader in firearm training, developing safe shooters through a network of certified instructors," NRA.org, accessed October 8, 2015, http://programs.nra.org.

19. James Hamblin, "The Question Doctors Can't Ask," *Atlantic*, August 11, 2014; James Palermo, "Law Upheld—Doctors Can't Ask Patients About Guns," *Space Coast Daily,* July 31, 2014; Michael Luojan, "N.R.A. Stymies Firearms Research, Scientists Say," *New York Times,* January 25, 2011; "Break the NRA's Ban on Gun-Violence Research," *Bloomberg View,* April 21, 2015; Todd C. Frankel, "Why the CDC Still Isn't Researching Gun Violence, Despite the Ban Being Lifted Two Years Ago," *Washington Post,* January 15, 2015.

20. $993 million in profit and $13 billion in revenues estimate from *Guns & Ammunition Manufacturing in the US: Market Research Report,* IBIS World, August 2015; $11 billion estimates from Statistics Brain Research Institute citing State Fish & Game Departments, Bureau of Alcohol, Tobacco, Firearms, and Explosives, IRS, July 2015.

Chapter 5

1. Sherwin Nuland, "The Extraordinary Power of Ordinary People," TED Talk, January 2009, https://www.ted.com/talks/sherwin_nuland_on_hope/transcript?language=en.

2. There was a study that suggested some kind of a relationship between dairy consumption and heart disease, but it has since been discredited for not adequately controlling for other relevant variables that may have compounded rates and incidence of heart disease: "Udder Confusion," *UC Berkeley School of Public Health Wellness Letter,* 2007.

3. Emma Green, "The Controversial Life of Skim Milk," *Atlantic*, November 20, 2013.

4. Roberto Ferdman, "The Mysterious Case of America's Plummeting Milk Consumption," *Washington Post,* June 20, 2014 (quoting data sourced from the USDA).

5. Ibid.

6. Emma Green, "The Controversial Life."

7. Mario Kratz, Ton Baars, Stephan Guyenet, "The Relationship Between High-Fat Dairy Consumption and Obesity, Cardiovascular, And Metabolic Disease." *European Journal of Nutrition.* February 2013; 52(1):1–24.

8. U.S. National Library of Medicine, National Institutes of Health.

9. Donna L. Hoyert, "75 Years of Mortality in the United States, 1935–2010." *National Center for Health Statistics Data Brief* No. 88 (2012).

10. As cited in "History of Eastern State Penitentiary," Eastern State Penitentiary, http://www.easternstate.org/history-eastern-state.

11. "In recognition of the psychological harm that can result from isolating people even for relatively brief periods, international human rights experts and organizations have called on governments to restrict their use of solitary confinement so that it is applied only in exceptional circumstances, for the shortest possible period of time": Amnesty International, "Entombed: Isolation in the US Federal Prison System," accessed September 18, 2015, http://www.amnestyusa.org/research/reports/entombed-isolation-in-the-us-federal-prison-system?page=2O. Other prison systems, such as that of the United Kingdom, have moved to other models that actually increase control and social interaction among "problem prisoners," a system which has been shown to be more effective, according to Atul Gawande, "Hellhole: The United States Holds Tens of Thousands of Inmates in Long-Term Solitary Confinement. Is This Torture?" *New Yorker*, March 30, 2009.

12. "Text Alternative for Breast Cancer: Mammography Statistics—2015," American Cancer Society, infographics, accessed September 20, 2015, http://www.cancer.org/research/infographicgallery/mammography-statistics-text-alternative.

13. Eric Sun, Anupam B. Jena, Darius Lakdawalla, et al, "The Contributions of Improved Therapy and Earlier Detection to Cancer Survival Gains, 1988–2000," *Forum for Health Economics and Policy* 13(2) Article 1 (2010), http://www.degruyter.com/view/j/fhep.2010.13.2/fhep.2010.13.2.1195/fhep.2010.13.2.1195.xml.

14. "Hormone Replacement Therapy's Effect on Breast Cancer Risk Changes Over Time," Breast Cancer.org, April 7, 2015.

15. Nancy Krieger, Jarvis T. Chen, and Pamela D. Waterman, "Decline in US Breast Cancer Rates After the Women's Health Initiative: Socioeconomic and Racial/Ethnic Differentials," *American Journal of Public Health* 100 (Supplement 1) (2010): S132–S139, http://www.ncbi.nlm.nih.gov/pmc/articles/PMC2837433/.

16. Charlie Schmidt, "5-Year Survival Data Not Always a Good Measure of Progress," *Journal of the National Cancer Institute* Volume 98, Issue 24 (2006): 1761; Aaron Carroll, "Why Survival Rate Is Not the Best Way to Judge Cancer Spending," *New York Times*, April 13, 2015.

17. Lydia E. Pace and Nancy L. Keating, "A Systematic Assessment of Benefits and Risks to Guide Breast Cancer Screening Decisions," *Journal of*

American Medical Association 311(13)(2014):1327–1335, http://jama
.jamanetwork.com/article.aspx?articleid=1853165.

18. Eric Sun, et al., "The Contributions of Improved Therapy"; "Decrease in
    Breast Cancer Rates Related to Reduction in Use of Hormone Replace-
    ment Therapy," press release, National Cancer Institute, Department
    of Health and Human Services, April 18, 2007, www.nih.gov/news/pr/
    apr2007/nci-18a.htm.

19. "How Can We Improve the Breast Cancer Screening Programme?" Can-
    cer Research UK, October 2012, http://scienceblog.cancerresearchuk
    .org/2012/10/30/how-can-we-improve-the-breast-cancer-screening
    -programme/.

20. *The Independent UK Panel on Breast Cancer Screening: Benefits and
    Harms of Breast Cancer Screening: An Independent Review*, a report
    jointly commissioned by Cancer Research UK and the Department of
    Health, England, October 2012.

21. Archie Bleyer H. and Gilbert Welch, "Effect of Three Decades of Screen-
    ing Mammography on Breast-Cancer Incidence," *New England Journal
    of Medicine* 367 (2012):1998–2005; David Gorski, "A Holiday Round
    in the Mammography Debate," *Science-Based Medicine*, November 26,
    2012, accessed September 15, 2015, https://www.sciencebasedmedicine
    .org/a-holiday-round-in-the-mammography-debate/.

22. Wendy Y. Chen, Bernard Rosner, Susan E. Hankinson, et al., "Moder-
    ate Alcohol Consumption During Adult Life, Drinking Patterns, and
    Breast Cancer Risk," *Journal of the American Medicine Association*
    306(17)(2011): 1884–1890; Nick Mulcahy, "US Women Not Interested
    in Alcohol as Breast Cancer Risk, *Medscape*, December 19, 2013, http://
    www.medscape.com/viewarticle/818078.

23. "Blake Mycoskie—The One for One Movement," *Brown Safe*, June
    2012, http://www.brownsafe.com/preservingtomorrow/blake-mycoskie
    -the-one-for-one-movement/.

24. "TOMS Company Overview," accessed September 23, 2015, www.
    toms.com.

25. Garth Frazer, "Used Clothing Donations and Apparel Production in
    Africa," *Economic Journal*, 118(532), October 2008, 1764–1784. [see
    http://www.utsc.utoronto.ca/mgmt/garth-frazer]

26. "The One-for-One Business Model: Avoiding Unintended Conse-
    quences," *Knowledge at Wharton,* February 16, 2015, http://knowl
    edge.wharton.upenn.edu/article/one-one-business-model-social-impact
    -avoiding-unintended-consequences/.

27. While one could argue some good has come from these programs (pris-
    ons became more sanitary, many women's lives were saved, and lots of

people have received shoes), they have also done real damage. Imagine how much better off we would have been if those efforts had invested in understanding whether their interventions were actually effective and tracked real impact from the outset.

28. Lois Beckett, "Why Don't We Know How Many People Are Shot Each Year in America?" *Propublica*, May 14, 2014.

29. "United States—Gun Facts, Figures and the Law," Gunpolicy.org, see http://www.gunpolicy.org/firearms/region/united-states; Drew Desilver, "A Minority of Americans Own Guns, but Just How Many Is Unclear," Pew Research Center, June 4, 2013; William J. Krouse, "Gun Control Legislation," *Congressional Research Services*, November 14, 2012, 8.

30. "Safe Storage and Gun Locks Policy Summary," Law Center to Prevent Gun Violence, August 21, 2015.

31. Ibid

32. Center for Disease Control, *FastStats*, http://www.cdc.gov/nchs/fastats/homicide and WISQARS (Web-based Injury Statistics Query and Reporting System) http://www.cdc.gov/injury/wisqars/; Michael Planty and Jennifer L. Truman, "Firearm Violence," Office of Justice Programs, Bureau of Justice Statistics, May 2013.

33. The 32 percent fatality rate is extrapolated based on dividing the estimated total number of people shot and injured by the total number of fatalities and estimates of the total number of people shot and injured. Estimates on the total number of people shot and injured sources are sourced from WISQAR—Web-based Injury and Query System data from the Center for Disease Control, cdc.org.

34. David Hemenway, "Guns, Suicide, and Homicide: Individual-Level Versus Population-Level Studies." *Annals of Internal Medicine* (2014).

35. Linda Dahlberg, Robin M. Ikeda, Marcie-Jo Kresnow, "Guns in the Home and Risk of a Violent Death in the Home: Findings from a National Study." *American Journal of Epidemiology* 160(10) (2004).

36. Michael Siegel, Craig S. Ross, "The Relationship Between Gun Ownership and Firearm Homicide Rates in the United States, 1981–2010." *American Journal of Public Health,* November 2013, Volume 103, No. 11.

37. "Firearm Deaths and Injuries in New York City." *Epi Research Report*, New York City Department of Health and Mental Hygiene, New York, April 2013.

38. Numbers by type of gun homicide are notoriously hard to estimate, but a national group tracking gang shootings estimates that there were one thousand gang-related firearm deaths in one year. Source: National Gang Center—National Youth Gang Survey Analysis, nationalgangcenter.gov, https://www.nationalgangcenter.gov/survey-analysis, accessed September

2015; Evan de Philipis, "Do We Have a Gang Problem or a Gun Problem?" *Huffington Post,* June 3, 2014, accessed October 8, 2015, http://www.huffingtonpost.com/evan-defilippis/do-we-have-a-gang-problem_b_5071639.html; Mass shootings are defined as shootings with more than four victims. In 2014, 385 people died in mass shootings, and domestic violence was a factor in many of these. (Especially murder-suicides.) Source: "Mass Shooting Tracker—Cited List of Known Mass Shootings", accessed September 30, 2015, http://shootingtracker.com/wiki/Mian_page

39. The estimate for four thousand lives saved is calculated by taking 20 percent of the average annual number of suicide fatalities (based on 5 years of data), a figure of approximately twenty thousand (sources: WISQARS Injury Data and Brady Campaign to Prevent Gun Violence).

Chapter 7

1. Eleanor Roosevelt, *You Learn by Living: Eleven Keys to a More Fulfilling Life*, Fiftieth Anniversary Edition (New York: Harper Perennial, 2011).

Chapter 8

1. This quote has been variously attributed to Leonardo da Vinci and others (although no known use appeared until 2000) and was the tagline for the Apple II advertising campaign. The earliest appearance in print seems to be attributable to Clare Boothe Brokaw (Clare Boothe Luce), *Stuffed Shirt* (New York: Horace Liveright, 1931), 239—though it appeared around the same time in a variety of forms.
2. Alain De Botton, *Status Anxiety* (Australia: Hamish Hamilton, 2004), 86.
3. Ibid, 88.
4. Deborah Hardoon, "Wealth: Having It All and Wanting More," *Oxfam Briefing Issue,* January 2015, http://policy-practice.oxfam.org.uk/publications/wealth-having-it-all-and-wanting-more-338125.
5. Steve Hargreaves, "The Myth of the American Dream," CNN Money, 2013, http://money.cnn.com/2013/12/09/news/economy/america-economic-mobility/; Elise Gould, "US Lags Behind Peer Countries in Mobility," *Economic Snapshot,* Economic Policy Institute, October 2012, http://www.epi.org/publication/usa-lags-peer-countries-mobility/.
6. Julia Isaacs, *International Comparisons of Economic Mobility*, Brookings Institution, 2008, brookings.edu.
7. Sentiment is shifting (twenty years earlier the number was 60 percent), and varies substantially by political affiliation—more than 60 percent of Democrats say forces outside an individual's control are the most significant cause of poverty, compared with just 27 percent of Republicans.

Source: Seth Freed Wessler, "Poll: Fewer Americans Blame Poverty on the Poor," NBC News, June 2014, http://www.nbcnews.com/feature/in-plain-sight/poll-fewer-americans-blame-poverty-poor-n136051.

8. Mark R. Rank, Yoon Hong-Sik, and Thomas A. Hirschl, "American Poverty as a Structural Failing: Evidence and Arguments," *Journal of Sociology & Social Welfare* Vol. 30, No. 4 (2003).

Chapter 9

1. Lisa Ordonez, Maurice Schweitzer, Adam Galinsky, et al., "Goals Gone Wild: The Systematic Side Effects of Over-Prescribing Goal Setting," working paper, Harvard Business School, 2009.

2. Frequently attributed to Winston Churchill, the first official recording of this quote seems to be a 2007 *Financial Times* obituary for U.K. Conservative politician Ian Gilmour (1926–2007), which stated he had used the line in a cabinet meeting in 1981, as noted in Barry Popik.com.

REFERENCES

Amnesty International. *Entombed: Isolation in the US Federal Prison System*. Amnesty International, 2015. http://www.amnestyusa.org/research/reports/entombed-isolation-in-the-us-federal-prison-system.

Anderson, Scott, "The Urge to End It All," *The New Yorker,* July 6, 2008.

Bachmann, Helen, "The Swiss Difference: A Gun Culture That Works." *Time* magazine, December 20, 2012.

Barrientos, Armando, and David Hulme. "Just Give Money to the Poor: The Development Revolution from the Global South," Presentation—Brooks World Poverty Institute, University of Manchester, U.K. 2010.

Beckett, Lois. "Why Don't We Know How Many People Are Shot Each Year in America?" *Propublica*, May 14, 2014.

Bleyer, Archie, and H. Gilbert Welch. "Effect of Three Decades of Screening Mammography on Breast-Cancer Incidence." *New England Journal of Medicine*, November 2012.

Bloomberg View. "Break the NRA's Ban on Gun-Violence Research." *Bloomberg View,* April 21, 2015.

Bornstein, David. *How to Change the World—Social Entrepreneurs and the Power of New Ideas*, New York, Oxford University Press, 2004.

BreastCancer.org. "Hormone Replacement Therapy's Effect on Breast Cancer Risk Changes Over Time." BreastCancer.org, April 7, 2015. http://www.breastcancer.org/research-news/hrt-and-breast-cancer-risk-changes-over-time.

Brown Safe. "Blake Mycoskie—The One for One Movement." http://www.brownsafe.com/preservingtomorrow/blake-mycoskie-the-one-for-one-movement/.

Cancer Research UK. "How Can We Improve the Breast Cancer Screening Programme?" October 30, 2012. http://scienceblog.cancerresearchuk.org/2012/10/30/how-can-we-improve-the-breast-cancer-screening-programme/.

Carroll, Aaron. "Why Survival Rate Is Not the Best Way to Judge Cancer Spending." *New York Times*, April 13, 2015.

Chen, Wendy Y., Bernard Rosner, Susan E. Hankinson, et al. "Moderate Alcohol Consumption During Adult Life, Drinking Patterns, and Breast Cancer Risk." *Journal of the American Medical Association* 306 (17) (2011): 1884–1890.

Child Trends Data Bank. "Teen Homicide, Suicide and Firearm Death—Indicators on Children and Youth." Child Trends Data Bank, March 2015.

Churchill, Winston. "We Shall Fight on the Beaches," speech to House of Commons, June 4, 1940, as cited by the Churchill Center.

Collins, Jerry C., and Jerry I. Porras. "Building Your Company's Vision." *Harvard Business Review*, September–October 1996.

—*Built to Last: Successful Habits of Visionary Companies.* New York: Harper Collins, 2011.

Cooper, Alexia, and Erica Smith. "Homicide Trends in the United States, 1980–2008—Annual Rates for 2009 and 2010," U.S. Department of Justice, Office of Justice Programs, Bureau of Justice Statistics, November 2011.

Council on Injury, Violence, and Poison Prevention Executive Committee. "Firearm-Related Injuries Affecting the Pediatric Population." *American Committee of Pediatrics*, November 1, 2012.

Cummings, Peter, David C. Grossman, Frederick P. Rivara, and Thomas D. Koepsell. "State Gun Safe Storage Laws and Child Mortality Due to Firearms." *The Journal of the American Medical Association*, Volume 278, No. 13 (1997).

Dahlberg, Linda, Robin M. Ikeda, Marcie-Jo Kresnow. "Guns in the Home and Risk of a Violent Death in the Home: Findings from a National Study." *American Journal Epidemiology* (2004).

Dalton, Amy, and Stephen Spiller. "Too Much of a Good Thing: The Benefits of Implementation Intentions Depend on the Number of Goals." *Journal of Consumer Research* Volume 39 (2012).

De Botton, Alain. *Status Anxiety*, Australia: Hamish Hamilton, Penguin Group Australia, 2004.

DeFilippis, Evan, and Devin Hughes. "Gun Deaths in Children: Statistics Show Firearms Endanger Kids Despite NRA Safety Programs." *Slate*, June 17, 2014.

Desilver, Drew. "A Minority of Americans Own Guns, but Just How Many Is Unclear." Pew Research Center, June 4, 2013.

Dweck, Carol. *Mindset: The New Psychology of Success.* New York: Ballantine Books, 2007.

Eastern State Penitentiary. "History of Eastern State Penitentiary." http://www.easternstate.org/learn/research-library/history.

Erbentraut, J. "Mothers Helped Troubled Neighborhood Stay Shooting-Free During Violent Chicago Weekend." *Huffington Post*, July 7, 2015.

Ferdman, Roberto. "The Mysterious Case of America's Plummeting Milk Consumption." *Washington Post*, June 20, 2014.

Follman, Mark, "These Women Are the NRA's Worst Nightmare." *Mother Jones*, October 2014.

Ford, Henry, and Ralph Waldo Trine. *An Intimate Talk on Life—the Inner Thing—the Things of the Mind and Spirit—and the Inner Powers and Forces that Make for Achievement*. Indiana: The Bobbs-Merrill Company, 1929.

Frankel, Todd C. "Why the CDC Still Isn't Researching Gun Violence, Despite the Ban Being Lifted Two Years Ago." *Washington Post*, January 15, 2015.

Frazer, Garth. "Used Clothing Donations and Apparel Production in Africa," *Economic Journal*, 118(532), October 2008, 1764–1784.

Gawande, Atul. "Hellhole: The United States Holds Tens of Thousands of Inmates in Long-Term Solitary Confinement. Is This Torture?" *New Yorker*, March 30, 2009.

Gorski, David. "A Holiday Round in the Mammography Debate." *Science-Based Medicine*, November 26, 2012.

Gould, Elise. "US Lags Behind Peer Countries in Mobility." *Economic Snapshot*, Economic Policy Institute, October 10, 2012.

Green, Emma. "The Controversial Life of Skim Milk." *Atlantic*, November 20, 2013.

GunPolicy.org. "United States—Gun Facts, Figures and the Law." GunPolicy .org, 2015.

Hamblin, James. "The Question Doctors Can't Ask." *Atlantic*, August 11, 2014.

Hardoon, Deborah. "Wealth: Having It All and Wanting More." *Oxfam Briefing Issue*, January 2015.

Hargreaves, Steve. "The Myth of the American Dream." *CNN Money*, 2013.

Hartnett, Daniel. "The Heuristics of Justice," Proceedings of the 65th Annual Meeting of the Jesuit Philosophical Association, 2004.

Harvard School of Public Health, "Bridges and Suicides." *Means Matter*, November 15, 2014. http://www.hsph.harvard.edu/means-matter/bridges -and-suicide/.

Heath, Chip, and Dan Heath. *Switch: How to Change Things When Change is Hard*. New York: Crown Business, 2010.

Henderson, D.A. Smallpox: The Death of a Disease—The Inside Story of Eradicating a Worldwide Killer. New York: Prometheus, 2009.

Hemenway, David. "Guns, Suicide, and Homicide: Individual-Level Versus Population-Level Studies." *Annals of Internal Medicine* 160(2) (2014).

Ho, Mandy, Sarah P. Garnett, and Louise Baur, et al. "Effectiveness of Lifestyle Interventions in Child Obesity: Systematic Review with Meta-analysis." *Pediatrics,* Volume 130 (2012).

Holan, Mark. "Ice Bucket Challenge Has Raised $220 Million Worldwide." *Washington Business Journal,* December 12, 2014.

Hoyert, Donna L. "75 Years of Mortality in the United States, 1935–2010." National Center for Health Statistics Data Brief, No 88, March 2012.

Huh S.Y., S.L. Rifas-Shiman, J.W. Rich-Edwards, E.M. Taveras, et al. "Prospective Association Between Milk Intake and Adiposity in Preschool-Aged Children." *Journal of the American Dietetic Association* 110(4) (2010).

IBISWorld. *Guns & Ammunition Manufacturing in the US: Market Research Report.* IBISWorld, August 2015.

Isaacs, Julia. *International Comparisons of Economic Mobility.* Brookings Institution, 2008.

Karch, Debra, Linda Dahlberg, and Nimesh Patel. "Surveillance for Violent Deaths—National Death Reporting System, 16 States, 2007." *Center for Diseases Control and Prevention—Morbidity and Mortality Weekly Report* 59(SS04) (2010): 1–50.

Kratz, Mario, Baars, Ton, and Guyenet Stephan, "The Relationship Between High-Fat Dairy Consumption and Obesity, Cardiovascular, And Metabolic Disease." *European Journal of Nutrition.* February 2013; 52(1):1–24.

Kirby, Emma Jane. "Switzerland Guns: Living with Firearms the Swiss Way." BBC News, February 11, 2013.

Klein, Ezra. "Mythbusting: Israel and Switzerland Are Not Gun-Toting Utopias." *Washington Post,* December 14, 2012.

Knowledge at Wharton. "The One-for-One Business Model: Avoiding Unintended Consequences." Wharton School at the University of Pennsylvania, 2015.

Kopel, David B., and Stephen D'Andrilli. "What America Can Learn from Switzerland Is That the Best Way to Reduce Gun Misuse Is to Promote Responsible Gun Ownership." *American Rifleman,* February 1990.

Krieger, Nancy, Jarvis T. Chen, and Pamela D. Waterman. "Decline in US Breast Cancer Rates After the Women's Health Initiative: Socioeconomic and Racial/Ethnic Differentials." *American Journal of Public Health,* 100 (Supplement 1) (2010): S132–S139.

Krouse, William J. "Gun Control Legislation." Congressional Research Services, November 14, 2012.

Latham, Gary P., and Edwin A. Locke. "New Developments in and Directions for Goal-Setting Research." *European Psychologists* Vol 12(4) (2007): 290–300.

Law Center to Prevent Gun Violence. *Safe Storage and Gun Locks Policy Summary.* Law Center to Prevent Gun Violence, August 2015.

Leventhal, John, Julie Gaither, and Robert Sege. "Hospitalizations Due to Firearm Injuries in Children and Adolescents." *Official Journal of American Academy of Pediatrics,* 2013.

Luce, Clare Boothe. *Snobs, New Style.* New York: Horace Liveright, 1931.

Luojan, Michael. "N.R.A. Stymies Firearms Research, Scientists Say." *New York Times,* January 25, 2011.

Miller, Matthew, Azrael, Deborah and Hemenway, David, "Belief in the Inevitability of Suicide: Results From A National Survey." *Suicide and Life Threatening Behavior,* 35:1–11, 2006

Miller, Matthew, and Hemenway, David, "Guns and Suicide in the United States," *The New England Journal of Medicine,* 359:989–991, 2008

Mothers Against Drunk Driving. "Drunk Driving Fatalities Fall Below 10,000." *MADD35,* December 10, 2012.

Mulcahy, Nick. "US Women Not Interested in Alcohol as Breast Cancer Risk." *Medscape,* December 19, 2013.

National Cancer Institute. "Decrease in Breast Cancer Rates Related to Reduction in Use of Hormone Replacement Therapy." Press release from Department of Health and Human Services, National Institute of Health News, April 18, 2007.

Neafsey, John. *A Sacred Voice Is Calling.* Maryknoll, NY: Orbis Books, 2006.

New York City Department of Health and Mental Hygiene, "Firearm Deaths and Injuries in New York City." *Epi Research Report,* New York, April 2013.

Nuland, Sherwin. "The Extraordinary Power of Ordinary People." Ted Talk, January 2009.

Ordonez, Lisa, Maurice Schweitzer, Adam Galinsky, et al. "Goals Gone Wild: The Systematic Side Effects of Over-Prescribing Goal Setting." Working paper, Harvard Business School, 2009.

Pace, L.E., and N.L. Keating. "A Systematic Assessment of Benefits and Risks to Guide Breast Cancer Screening Decisions." *Journal of American Medical Association* 311(13) (2014):1327–1335.

Palermo, James. "Law Upheld—Doctors Can't Ask Patients About Guns." *Space Coast Daily,* July 31, 2014.

Palmer, Edith. "Firearms-Control Legislation and Policy: Switzerland." Law Library of Congress, February 2013.

Perry, James L. *The Jossey-Bass Reader on Nonprofit and Public Leadership.* New York: Jossey-Bass, 2010.

Pew Research Center. "Gun Homicide Rate Down 49% Since 1993 Peak; Public Unaware—Pace of Decline Slows in Past Decade." Pew Research Center, May 2013.

Planty, Michael, and Jennifer L. Truman. "Firearm Violence." Office of Justice Programs, Bureau of Justice Statistics, May 2013.

Rank, Mark R., Hong-Sik Yoon, and Thomas A. Hirschl. "American Poverty as a Structural Failing: Evidence and Arguments." *Journal of Sociology & Social Welfare,* December 2003.

Roosevelt, Eleanor. *You Learn by Living: Eleven Keys to a More Fulfilling Life,* Fiftieth Anniversary Edition. New York: Harper Perennial, 2011.

Russakoff, Dale. *The Prize: Who's in Charge of America's Schools?* New York: Houghton Mifflin Harcourt, 2015.

Sanburn, Josh. "America's Gun Economy, By the Numbers." *Time* magazine, December 8, 2012.

Schmidt, Charlie. "5-Year Survival Data Not Always a Good Measure of Progress." *Journal of the National Cancer Institute* Volume 98, Issue 24 (2006): 1761.

Siegel, Michael, Craig S. Ross, and Charles King II. "The Relationships Between Gun Ownership and Firearm Homicide Rates in the United States, 1981–2010," *American Journal of Public Health* Volume 103, No. 11 (2013).

Simon, Stacy. "Report: Cancer Death Rates Decline, but More Slowly Among Poor." American Cancer Society, October 3, 2011.

Sun, Eric, Anupam B. Jena, Darius Lakdawalle, et al. "The Contributions of Improved Therapy and Earlier Detection to Cancer Survival Gains, 1988–2000." *Forum for Health Economics and Policy* 13(2) Article 1 (2010).

The Independent UK Panel on Breast Cancer Screening. *Benefits and Harms of Breast Cancer Screening: An Independent Review.* Report jointly commissioned by Cancer Research UK and the Department of Health, England, October 2012.

Thomas, Dennis. "20 U.S. Kids Hospitalized Each Day for Gun Injuries." *HealthDay News,* January 2014.

UC Berkeley School of Public Health. "Udder Confusion." *UC Berkeley School of Public Health Wellness Letter,* 2007.

United States Center for Disease Control. "Parasites—Hookworm." Centers for Disease Control, January 10, 2013.

Wang, Youfa, Yang Wu, Renee F. Wilson, et al. "Childhood Obesity Prevention Programs: Comparative Effectiveness Review," Agency for Health Care Research and Quality, US Department of Health and Human Services, June 2013.

Wessler, Seth Freed. "Poll: Fewer Americans Blame Poverty on the Poor." NBCnews.com, June 2014.

INDEX

ABOUT THE AUTHOR

Liana Downey is an internationally recognized strategic advisor, speaker, and author dedicated to creating social change. As executive director of Liana Downey & Associates, Downey leads a global team that helps leaders and organizations increase focus and change lives. Clients include social enterprises, global nonprofits, and federal, state, and city governments such as the Community Resources Exchange, Speak up Africa, Community Solutions, the Nature Conservancy, the NYC Education Department, Children's Aid Society, and the Administration for Children's Services.

Previously, Downey was a leader of the nonprofit and government practices at McKinsey & Company in Australia, a special strategic advisor to the Australian Department of Prime Minister and Cabinet, and a commercial advisor on the Baku-Tblisi gas pipeline negotiations in Tblisi, Georgia.

Downey holds an MBA from Stanford (Arjay Miller Scholar), lectures at the NYU John F. Wagner Graduate School of Public Service in New York, and is on the Board of Room to Grow, an innovative nonprofit dedicated to improving the lives of families living with poverty.

Downey lives with her husband and children in New York.